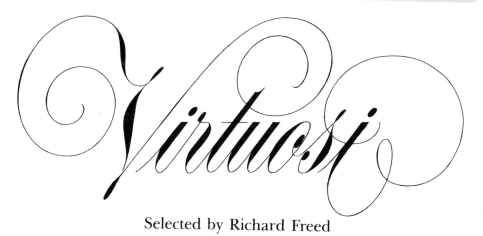

Virtuosi

Selected by Richard Freed

The Smithsonian Collection of Recordings
Washington DC
1985

The Smithsonian Collection of Recordings
is a division of the Smithsonian Institution Press,
Felix C. Lowe, Director.

Executive Producer: J.R. Taylor
Associate Producer: Margaret Robinson
Booklet Editor: Jane Sapp
Mastering Engineer: Steven Smolian
Designer: Stephen Kraft
Source recordings from the participating record companies
Special thanks to Kathryn King and Elizabeth Eaton

Photographs of the performers from EMI Records, Ltd.;
International Piano Archives at Maryland; and the
Music Division, New York Public Library at Lincoln
Center, Astor, Lenox, and Tilden Foundations

Contents

Program

SIDE 1 **PABLO CASALS, cello**
1. BACH: Cello Suite no. 3 in C major, BWV 1009[1]
WANDA LANDOWSKA, harpsichord
2. BACH: Italian Concerto in F major, BWV 971[1]

SIDE 2 **JOSEPH SZIGETI, violin**
London Philharmonic Orchestra,
Sir Thomas Beecham cond.
1. PROKOFIEV: Violin Concerto no. 1 in D major, op. 19[1]

SIDE 3 **ALFRED CORTOT, piano**
1. SCHUMANN: Kinderszenen, op. 15[1]
LÉON GOOSSENS, oboe; members of the Léner Quartet
2. MOZART: Oboe Quartet in F major, K. 370[1]

SIDE 4 **ARTUR SCHNABEL, piano**
London Symphony Orchestra,
Sir Malcolm Sargent cond.
1. MOZART: Piano Concerto no. 21 in C major, K. 467[1]

SIDE 5 **ARTHUR RUBINSTEIN, piano**
1. FAURÉ: Nocturne in A-flat major, op. 33, no. 3[1]
2. POULENC: Mouvements perpetuels[1]
3. CHOPIN: Three Nocturnes, op. 9[1]
4. FALLA: "Ritual Fire Dance" from *El Amor brujo*[1]

SIDE 6 **YEHUDI MENUHIN, GEORGE ENESCU, violins**
Paris Symphony Orchestra,
Pierre Monteux cond.
1. BACH: Concerto in D minor for Two Violins, BWV 1043[1]
DINU LIPATTI, piano
2. CHOPIN: Waltz in C-sharp minor, op. 64, no. 2[1]
Waltz in A-flat major, op. 64, no. 3[1]
Waltz in F minor, op. 70, no. 2[1]
Waltz in D-flat major, op. 70, no. 3[1]
Grande Valse brillante in E-flat major, op. 18[1]

SIDE 7 **EMANUEL FEUERMANN, cello**
Philadelphia Orchestra,
Leopold Stokowski cond.
1. BLOCH: Schelomo[2]
GREGOR PIATIGORSKY, cello; SOLOMON, piano
2. BEETHOVEN: Sonata for Cello and Piano, op. 102, no. 1[1]

6

SIDE 8   **WILLIAM PRIMROSE, viola; WILLIAM KAPELL, piano**
1. BRAHMS: Viola Sonata, op. 120, no. 1[2]

WALTER GIESEKING, piano
2. BRAHMS: Intermezzo in B minor, op. 119, no. 1[1]
Intermezzo in A major, op. 118, no. 2[1]

SIDE 9   **WALTER GIESEKING, piano**
1. DEBUSSY: Suite bergamasque[1]

DENNIS BRAIN, French horn
Philharmonia Orchestra,
Herbert von Karajan cond.
2. MOZART: Horn Concerto no. 3 in E-flat major, K. 447[1]

SIDE 10   **RUDOLF SERKIN, piano; Busch Quartet**
1. SCHUMANN: Piano Quintet in E-flat major, op. 44[3]

SIDE 11   **NATHAN MILSTEIN, violin; VLADIMIR HOROWITZ, piano**
1. BRAHMS: Violin Sonata no. 3 in D minor, op. 108[2]

REGINALD KELL, clarinet
Unidentified orchestra, Walter Goehr cond.
2. WEBER: Clarinet Concertino in E-flat major, op. 26[1]

SIDE 12   **FRITZ KREISLER, violin**
Berlin State Opera Orchestra,
Leo Blech cond.
1. MENDELSSOHN: Violin Concerto in E minor, op. 64[1]

FRITZ KREISLER, violin
Carl Lamson, piano
2. KREISLER: Liebesleid[2]

SIDE 13   **SERGEI RACHMANINOFF, piano**
1. SCHUMANN: Carnaval, op. 9[2]

SIDE 14   **JASCHA HEIFETZ, violin**
London Philharmonic Orchestra,
Sir Thomas Beecham cond.
1. SIBELIUS: Violin Concerto in D minor, op. 47[1]

Included through the courtesy of: (1) EMI Records, Ltd., (2) RCA Records,
(3) CBS Special Products.

Foreword

Since its inception during the 1890s, the recorded music industry has devoted most of its energies to the works of active performers, which fact should neither surprise nor mystify. Novelty for its own sake, though it may come in the unlikely guise of the nth recording of a symphony by Tchaikovsky, will always have its claim. Performers of genuine gifts continue to appear; understandably, their concerts, recitals, broadcasts, lectures, writings, American Express commercials—even their reclusions, as in the case of the late Glenn Gould—tend to draw more attention to their growing discographies than is given to those of their senior colleagues who have retired or died. The fidelity of the recording process, which has been enhanced in stages through nearly a century of technological advances, also weighs increasingly upon our perception of now inactive musicians. All other things being identical, a 1985 compact disc recording will give a more truthful performance picture than would its stereophonic analog counterpart from 1965, which in turn would be more accurate than a 1950 record from a monaural tape master, itself a step closer to actuality than the 1930s direct-to-disc electrical recordings, which supplanted the still less realistic acoustical pioneers from the first quarter of our century.

The performances in *Virtuosi* were recorded over a period of three decades, beginning during the twilight of the acoustical era and concluding shortly before the commercial application of stereophony. Some of these interpretations are so celebrated that they have remained available since their first day in release, but for the most part, these recordings have spent many of the years since the advent of stereo as collector's items, surfacing for a few years at a time as domestic or hard-to-find imported re-issues. For several, *Virtuosi* provides their first appearances in decades, or even their first ever on LP. As a group, they comprise a survey of many of the most distinguished and distinctive instrumentalists of their time. That time did not know the directionality of stereo or the ranges of frequency and dynamics provided by later developments, but this collection clearly demonstrates that it did not want for exceptional soloists.

9

The listener who can only be satisfied by today's technical standards in recording will take little pleasure in *Virtuosi*. Nevertheless, regardless of the sophistication of the equipment at their disposal, recording engineers have always tried to reflect the strengths of the performances born in their presences. The adventurous listener may wish to proceed directly to the very earliest recording here, Fritz Kreisler's acoustical Mendelssohn Violin Concerto, for an example of how well they have sometimes done. Here is a wild and inimitable tone, captured by a device less complex than a mousetrap. For our part, we have simply attempted to restore the original sound of these classic recordings as faithfully as possible, using the best available source materials.

In his introductory essay, Peter Eliot Stone points out that the period from the 1920s into the 1950s saw a reconsideration of the soloist's role, as part of a larger and still ongoing shift in musical values toward more faithful realization of the composer's intentions. As one might expect in any living art form, this shift has occurred gradually, producing a number of anachronisms as it went. Wanda Landowska performed the works of Scarlatti, Handel, and (as here) Bach on the harpsichord, but the instrument she favored was a rather distant relative of any harpsichord that those composers knew. Pablo Casals rediscovered Bach's cello suites and reintroduced them in irreplaceable performances; these performances, however, were conceived in a style based on the literature of the nineteenth century, perhaps in part because much of the specific meaning of mid-eighteenth-century notation had been forgotten during the century prior to Casals's birth. Fritz Busch's 1936 recording of the Second Brandenburg Concerto used a specially built trumpet to accommodate the high notes that previous conductors, sensible of their difficulty, had pragmatically assigned to a clarinet; yet the newly built trumpet was a modification of the twentieth-century instrument rather than a replica of the valveless instrument of Bach's day, and the rest of Busch's orchestra was altogether modern in its instrumentation. Artur Schnabel was celebrated for strictly harnessing his interpretive wisdom to the composer's wishes, but in his performance of the Mozart concerto heard here, he is accompanied by an edition of the London Symphony Orchestra that still perpetuated the nineteenth-century practice of *portamento* by sliding up to certain notes from below; the effect is as curious to the listener of the 1980s as it would have been to Mozart.

Authenticity in performance style is slippery to the grasp, for regardless of the amount of documentation available to the scholar-performer, generalities must always be drawn from the particular. If we assume that any composition can be realized in a somehow ideal performance, a model for other performances in every detail of tempo and dynamics and phrasing, recordings contradict us; time and again, a composer has conducted or supervised successive and significantly different recorded versions of one of his works. Yet there can be little doubt that the movement toward careful research into authentic performance practice and appropriate use of antique instruments (and their replicas) has enriched today's musical life. For a century, most performers on original instruments were considered pedants, or purists in a negative sense; today they are more commonly seen simply as that group of musicians—some excellent, others indifferent, as in any other field—who deepen our understanding and enjoyment of masterworks by presenting them in the terms familiar to their composers and first performers. To most listeners to this collection, it may be of particular interest that American-born musicians specializing in this field can be considered, for the first time in the history of European concert music, to have achieved a parity of excellence with their European colleagues; Smithsonian Collection releases by the Smithsonian Chamber Players and the Aston Magna Festival Orchestra stand alongside numerous recordings by other groups to support this view.

The present collection (unlike those mentioned just above) does not, and by its very nature could not, claim to present a demonstration of the best current opinions on performance practice for the eighteenth-century (and, in a number of cases, the nineteenth-century) works included here. Thanks to the knowledge and discernment of Richard Freed, it can claim to offer a representative overview of outstanding figures from the second quarter of our century, when a different range of musical ideals prevailed all but unquestioned. In a very real sense, original instruments performers are revolutionaries; they understand music somewhat differently than did many performers of earlier generations. In the end, however, the integrity of the impulse toward music-making can transcend as well as encompass scholarship, as the performances in *Virtuosi*, whether heard for pleasure alone or as an aid to perspective on the changing world of music, will show.

11

The Virtuoso in History

The word "virtuoso" acts like one of those sub-atomic particles recently discovered by nuclear physicists: instead of behaving predictably as would, say, any classically conceived electron, now it is here, now it is there (or both, or neither), and its charge may be positive or negative (or both), dependent not only upon itself but also upon the context in which it exists and the way it or its context is perceived by observers. Put proverbially, one man's meat is another man's poison.

Some musicians utter the word "virtuoso" with the contempt usually reserved for "critic" or "manager." The objects of their contempt are performers who totally subjugate a work and the intentions of its composer to their desire or need to show off their agility or performers who, consciously or unconsciously avoiding wholesale violation of art works, debauch their audiences by only playing superficially brilliant or mawkish pieces, on the theory that exhibitionism will win them over. The resultant pejorative connotation, fixed in the minds of those for whom music is paramount, does not jibe with performers who put their technical mastery at the service of music. But even empty virtuosity can create techniques that, in the proper hands, will expand expressive possibilities for both composer and performer: the remarkable performer, the virtuoso, can fertilize as well as kill music. Perhaps this explains both the extraordinary esteem in which some players are held and the peculiar sense of values by which audiences prize performers above composers. A number of years ago, when the pianist originally scheduled to give the première of an American piano concerto with a major American orchestra had to withdraw because of illness, the composer himself played the work. He returned from the performance, complaining to his composition class: "I was paid more for playing the work than for writing it."

The fame of many musicians' virtuosity has often obscured their own greater merit as composers. Franz Liszt had to die before his truly important compositions would become known; the deliciously scandalous image of the amorist and the glitter of his Hungarian Rhapsodies hid the innovative late works from public view. Similarly, not many people know the numerous symphonies, suites, violin concerto, opera, sonatas, quartets, songs, and other works of George Enescu, which were outshone by the dazzle of his virtuosic violin playing; yet he considered himself first and foremost a composer.

Of virtuosi, the kind that most irrationally captures the imagination of the public is—pejorative of pejoratives—the prodigy. Actually, most composers (and virtuosi) were prodigies, that is, early bloomers. Generalizations about prodigies abound and most of them are false. Prodigies are not rare, nor is their exploitation (or that of their audiences) rare; their number is prodigious. There is hardly a composer or performer one can name who did not start doing amazing things long before his or her tenth birthday. The most precocious of all was William Crotch (1775–1847) who, at two years and three weeks, discovered on the organ, guided only by instinct, the harmonization of "God Save the King." He eventually (and appropriately) became director of the Royal Academy of Music.

As a rule, prodigies do not die early; in fact, some of the longest-lived musicians began as prodigies. Nor do they burn out at an early age.

Their development as musical artists does not hinder their development as human beings, nor does that development necessarily make them narrow. Many prodigies grew up to be theorists, philosophers, critics, mathematicians, chemists, chess masters, and letter writers who often elegantly expressed themselves in several languages as well as in music. Their personalities do not fall into any one category: onstage they may have been placid, childlike (until they performed), confident, solemn, playful, demonic, intense, polite, or transfixed.

The word "virtuoso" comes from the Latin *virtus,* which means excellence, worth. It characterizes a person of exceptional attainment and, when applied to a musician, implies extraordinary technical skill in the practice of his instrument. In its sixteenth- and seventeenth-century Italian usage, however, it emphasized creative and intellectual genius rather than aptitude for dexterity and performance, whether in poetry, architecture, or music. Thus a musical virtuoso had to be a skillful composer and theorist or at least a *maestro di cappella.*

In the late seventeenth and early eighteenth centuries many Italian musicians went north, applying the term "virtuoso" to themselves whether or not they knew theory or composition. Perhaps that is why Johann Mattheson had to differentiate between *theoretische Virtuosen* and *virtuosi prattici* as early as 1720. Twenty years before that, Johann Kuhnau opposed the true virtuoso to the *musicus,* who was merely a performer. However, by the late eighteenth century the wandering Italians had their way, and instrumental soloists, castrati, and solo sopranos all described themselves as virtuosi. As attitudes toward "athletic" performances became positive, the term became equivocal, and Liszt felt it necessary to point out that "virtuosity is not an outgrowth but an indispensable element of music." Richard Wagner did not really disagree: "The real dignity of the virtuoso rests solely on the dignity he is able to preserve for creative art; if he trifles and toys with this, he casts his honor away. He is the intermediary of the artistic idea."

Clearly, semantic difficulties arise, owing to the history of the term and to the conflicting values that individuals bring to different kinds of performance in different eras. Initially, the words "virtuoso" and "composer" were almost synonymous, in that most great performers were also composers; composition and performance derived from a common source. But as these musical roles separated and became specialized, one tended to think of composers *contra* performers. (Yet this distinction had also bothered St. Augustine, who compared mere performers with beasts.) Now, performers of acrobatic temperament, who perform insignificant music or good music that they destroy with cheap tricks, are often called virtuosi. But the term "virtuoso" is also applied to the performer who sticks to the text and perfectly realizes the composer's intentions.

Furthermore, "virtuoso" in modern usage frequently connotes technical mastery. Is "technical mastery" the ability to play all the notes cleanly, in tune, and so on, at breakneck speed but without expressing the intent of the composer? What kind of mastery is it that does not perform the task for which it is designed? Is it not technical mastery then to reveal the composer's meaning even though some notes are misplayed? And if all the notes are properly played at breakneck speed but they belong to a meretricious, pretentious, or trifling work that panders to an audience, of what value is a technique that expresses nothing worthwhile? Is it improper to enjoy breathtaking feats, vertiginous acrobatics, and pyrotechnics for themselves? There is no "right" answer to these questions, but one's answer will put one down on one side or another of a controversy that has existed throughout the history of music.

The conditions under which virtuosi played have changed through

15

the ages; concerts or recitals as we know them (disregarding matters of taste) have existed only since the mid-nineteenth century. We can only conjecture about pre-history, but from the Fourth Millenium the Sumero-Chaldean and then Assyrian kings and wealthy subjects heard choruses and soloists at religious and military ceremonies and at banquets. Greek musicians in Plato's time held contests. Little is known about secular music in subsequent ages until about the tenth century A.D. when *goliards* (wandering students and clerics), *jongleurs* (itinerant fiddlers, singers, jugglers, and acrobats), and, in the twelfth and thirteenth centuries, *troubadours* and *trouvères* (Provençal and northern French gentleman-poets and composers), who wrote for their minstrels (*jongleurs*-in-residence), began to people the musico-historic stage. The nobility began to learn how to perform music, and iconography illustrates for us their tournaments, marriages, and regal entries, accompanied by an increasingly larger number of instruments.

After the Middle Ages vocal music became increasingly elaborate in the liturgy, and with the addition of instruments, concerts (in a very broad sense) can be said to have taken place in the churches, where organ recitals (likewise broadly interpreted) had already been heard. Intimate secular concerts came into vogue about the fourteenth century, some accompanying dinners. By the sixteenth century, music of the highest quality accompanied, with appropriate instrumental diversity, the seven or eight courses of sumptuous banquets.

Throughout the sixteenth century, academies (clubs that brought intellectuals together for discussion) flourished; Cosimo de' Medici founded the first, Plato's Academy, in Florence ca. 1460. Most academies also assembled composers, singers, and instrumentalists for entertainment. Some clubs were exclusively musical, charged annual dues, and hired a *maestro di musica* to teach singing and playing and to write music for their particular club. In 1570 Jean-Antoine de Baïf and Joachim Thibaut de Courville founded the first Parisian Academy of Poetry and Music; they provided for a concert every Sunday and charged dues, thereby forming one of the first private subscription societies. As academies, or as *collegia musica* in the German and Low Countries, the clubs spread across Europe.

The seventeenth century saw a burgeoning of church recitals and private concerts. The church recitals were open to the public, but it has been argued that music was secondary to the liturgical service.

16

A fifteenth-century banquet scene with musical accompaniment on the harp, fiddle, and portative organ. Miniature; Musée du Petit Palais, Paris

This seems not to be true when one considers, for example, the performance duels that took place, say between Girolamo Frescobaldi and Costantini in 1608 at St. Peter's in Rome. Perhaps good taste and the respect for consecrated ground somewhat disciplined the performers' desire to shine, but read what Frescobaldi wrote about playing a toccata: "Before playing a run in sixteenth notes for two hands, stop for a moment on the preceding note, even if it is short. Then resolutely play the run, thus showing to the best advantage the agility of your hands." Two centuries later in 1801, did the congregation at the church of San Martino in Lucca attend to God or to Paganini in his twenty-eight-minute concerto performed between the *Kyrie* and *Gloria* of the Mass?

Unlike the churches, the academies and collegia were restricted to the *cognoscenti*. But in the final years of the sixteenth century, a small academy, or *ridotto,* the so-called Florentine Camerata of Count

Giovanni de' Bardi, which included a few aristocrats, musicians, poets, and scientists, had adopted a purportedly classicistic aesthetic that gave rise to a new genre, opera. Initially for the pleasure of the aristocracy, the new genre achieved such popularity that the first public opera house was built; it opened in Venice in 1637 to the first public musical audience in a modern sense.

In the following years soloists, e.g. trumpets, of the Venetian opera house would provide divers flourishes during the overtures. In the French opera orchestra of Jean-Baptiste Lully, woodwind trios played against the large string body, thus offering a kind of concertino against the tutti. Similarly, solo writing in the Neapolitan operas of Alessandro Scarlatti was sometimes equal to that of a concerto. In London's Italian opera from 1715 to 1717, the violinist Francesco Veracini virtuosically entertained between acts and scenes. (Well into the nineteenth century, solo players at the Paris Opéra were differentiated from first-desk players or concertmasters: their only function was to play solos; they were excused from all routine duty.)

One of the most important developments in the history of music began in a very small way when, on 30 September 1672, John Bannister, composer and former first violin of the Royal Chamber Orchestra, initiated in his London home the first of a series of paid concerts. On their cessation in 1678, Thomas Britton, a "small coal" merchant and self-taught bibliophile, chemist, occultist, and gambist, continued Bannister's plan in a loft over the coal shop. Continued until 1714, his series was attended by the London elite, who themselves made music or heard most of the popular masters of the day. Handel was a regular in 1711. Open-air concerts followed in Vauxhall in 1732 and then in other London parks, in which were heard many of Handel's concertos. (In 1765, the year after Mozart "played" London's elegant pleasure garden Ranelagh, the fickle public had lost interest in him—he performed at the Swan and Hoop Tavern, in Cornhill.) J.C. Bach and C.F. Abel inaugurated their famous concert series (1764–82). (J.C. Bach reputedly gave the first solo piano recital, in 1768 in London.) In just a few years, the impresario Salomon's concerts would flourish, assisted by Haydn's presence. By the nineteenth century London had the most active, diversified, and specialized concert life in Europe.

In Paris, religious observance suspended musical performances at the Opéra on about thirty-five days a year. The flutist-composer, Anne-Danican Philidor, brother of composer and chess master

François-André-Danican Philidor, purchased a concession to perform "chapel music" for moderate prices in the Tuileries on those days, beginning on 18 March 1725. These *Concerts spirituels* he expanded by two weekly concerts in winter and one in summer in which secular music would also be allowed. Until the Revolution, virtuosi from all over Europe tried to perform in this series that was to launch many careers. From the 1730s to the 1750s, one of the farmers-general of Louis XV, Alexandre-Joseph de La Pouplinière, played Maecenas to many artists whose careers he helped launch, in part with private concerts at his mansion.

The Italians arrived with their concerti, but by the time of Mozart and Beethoven, Paris had become the home of a specifically French concerto style manifest in the work of Giovanni Battista Viotti, his student Jacques-Pierre-Joseph Rode, and Rodolphe Kreutzer. The popularity of the *Concerts spirituels* encouraged musicians in other European countries to set up similar series.

The impresario type of public concert flourished between 1710 and 1720 in Strasbourg, Augsburg, Bern, Lyons, Bologna, and Rome; important series developed at Frankfurt (1723), Leipzig (1743), Berlin (1745), Vienna (1771), and in the final thirty years of the century in medium- to small-sized cities. Private concerts, recitals, and chamber music sessions mushroomed and nourished virtuosi. (In the New World, musicians were not far behind their continental counterparts: in the late 1780s Alexander Reinagle organized a series of subscription concerts in New York and then set up a similar series that ran simultaneously in Philadelphia.) Though concerts did not yet have the shape of those we are used to, a general picture has emerged against which the development of the virtuoso can be observed.

The real virtuoso appears on the scene quite early. Bards had used the kithara, a boxed lyre associated with the cult of Apollo (which would give birth to the Classical aesthetic), in pre-Classical times. A thousand years later, in Classical times (sixth to fourth century B.C.), it was still used, writes Curt Sachs in *The History of Musical Instruments,* by professional musicians "when they had degenerated into capricious and intriguing virtuosi who, at exorbitant fees, performed in public theatres where adoring ladies would snatch away their plectra as highly prized souvenirs."

In 586 B.C. the elaborately dressed Sakadas of Argos played the aulos, a double oboe associated with the cult of Dionysus (which would give birth to the Romantic aesthetic), in its first appearance at

19

A maiden, possibly a Muse, playing the kithara. Bowl,
fifth century B.C.; Musée de Louvre, Paris

the Pythian games at Delphi and won the prize for his music descriptive of the battle between Apollo and the Python. Certain players of the aulos, whose music was more descriptive and less subtle than that for the earlier kithara, "were renowned and feted more than a Horowitz, an Oistrakh, a Callas," writes Marc Pincherle in *The World of the Virtuoso.* As the aulos players traveled from city to city they received huge amounts of money and gave lessons to the few students who could afford them. Sumptuous clothes and jewels dazzled the eyes, and descriptive music the ears, of the populace. Even in those days one spoke of professional degeneration, ostentatious dress, and the placement of claques in audiences.

In subsequent centuries and into the High Middle Ages, quasi-historic, quasi-legendary artists, singers, harpists, and the like peopled the world from Erin to Islam; they were dressed in colorful garments, accoutred with valuable jewels, attended by slaves, and, on their deaths, lamented as national treasures by king and caliph. At least as early as the twelfth century, the instrumentalist understood the value of skill, rapidity, liveliness, rhythmic precision, delicacy,

Aulos player and singer. Goblet, ca. 480 B.C.; Staatliche Antikensammlung, München

sweetness, and the dissimulation of that skill. The great Francesco Landini (1325-97), blind Florentine organist—of the organetto, i.e., portative organ—and composer, was described at work by a contemporary: "He starts to play with incomparable skill and great sweetness and, although deprived of the light of his eyes, with such speed that he surpasses all other organists whom one can remember."

The treatment of virtuosi after the fifteenth century suggests that they were the continuators of the *jongleurs* and minstrels. Conrad Paumann, blind like Landini, played various string and wind instruments but was primarily the virtuoso organist at the Cathedral in Munich. About 1470 he visited Ferrara, Mantua, and Milan, where he was paid with clothes, bolts of silk and velvet, and a sword.

In the sixteenth century, virtuosi mastered two instruments in particular: viola da gamba and lute. At first, they accompanied singers and improvised; later they only performed on the instruments as they went from court to court.

Almost no Italian keyboard music has come down to us from the fifteenth century despite its production in the fourteenth and efflores-

21

cence in the sixteenth centuries. The highly reputed Swiss-German organist, Paul Hofhaimer (1459–1537) knew the major musicians of his time in the influential Hapsburg court, yet the few works of his that are extant do not support that reputation. These and other apparent deviations from what one would logically expect lead to the supposition that improvised music was more highly valued than composed music.

The art of improvisation is important to the history of Western written music at least as far back as fourteenth-century English descant, in which a singer improvised his part against a pre-existent (written) one. Improvisation, like virtuosity, must have originated in the most primitive musical environment. The improvisatory and virtuosic instincts are symbiotically related, for the performer, recognizing that a potential of his instrument has not been realized, extemporizes and creates techniques capable of achieving that potential. This new technical mastery itself permits higher flights of imagination that, eventually being frustrated, will require yet newer techniques.

Preluding, playing to test or give tuning, these are formless extemporizations. A structure already exists in the case of the theme and variations which constitutes another source of improvisation and composition. Ornamentation, of either a note, a phrase, or a section, was not, in certain eras, merely decorative improvisation, certainly not in the Baroque, when it functioned as an essential means of expression.

Still another form suitable as a basis for improvisation was available when Italian gambists, lutenists, or organists transcribed a French vocal work, the polyphonic *chanson*. Their fingers told them that they did not have to play only the notes that had been sung; their fingers could do things that voices could not. The instrumentalists then combined the older vocal polyphonic discourse with the chords, arpeggios, trills, and runs of the newer instrumental homophonic one in the dexterously playful activity of the *canzona francese*. Eventually they created original, idiomatic works for their instruments. Thus, a genre in its infancy gradually separated itself from the one upon which it had been dependent, first differentiating itself, then becoming specialized, or idiomatic. In its expressive and technical maturity it turned again to other genres in order to borrow ideas for its own further enrichment.

These geographic, linguistic, temporal, and generic journeys brought about many transformations in the history of forms and styles. The austere German violin school, for example, had been imbued with the singing Italian aesthetic while emulating the polyphonic idiom of North German organ music in the late seventeenth century. Later, J.S. Bach, an eighteenth-century German organist, learned from North German violin music, as well as from Vivaldi's Italianate approach, and fused them with French harpsichord style. About sixty-five years ago—to make a small historic leap—Stravinsky was criticized for writing violin parts as if they were for trumpet; today, those parts are considered perfectly idiomatic.

What is "natural" for an instrument may simply mean what is conventional, not what is possible or even "correct." In the Baroque era, violin and trumpet-like cornetto, or Zink, parts were interchangeable. Even the natural (that is, valveless) trumpet, or clarin, parts in sonatas by the violin virtuoso Giuseppe Torelli could be played by violin. Torelli, a member of the Bolognese school famous for its trumpet sonatas, was an important innovator of the solo concerto and concerto grosso. It should not be surprising then to hear that Heinrich von Biber wrote as well for virtuoso trumpet as he did for virtuoso violin. Clearly, the criticism of Stravinsky arose from the failure of imagination on the part of the instrumentalist and critic and from their ignorance of the history of the repertory and of its performance practice.

Until the seventeenth century, vocal music predominated while instrumental music played a decidedly secondary role. In the seventeenth century, however, instrumental music came into its own, and while vocal music remained important—that was, after all, the century in which opera was launched—instrumentalists pullulated all over Europe, then pulled up their roots and, despite primitive transportation, seemed to be sown across the continent by the wind. Their personalities, provenances, destinations, contributions, instruments, genres, and chronology cross-pollinized music and produced a complex from which only arbitrary details can be plucked and fewer discussed in this limited space.

Because the violin had generally been played by fiddlers and lackeys in the sixteenth century, we know little about its masters. The first name that stands out is Baldassarino da Belgiojoso (or Balthazar de Beaujoyeulx), who, as Italian ballet master to Queen Louise, directed the celebrated *ballet de cour, Ballet comique de la Reine,* in 1581. And it is perhaps more than emblematic that the first known name is Italian, for with the exception of the Austrian Jakob Stainer (1621–83), all major makers of the classical violin were from northern Italy. Cremona boasted Niccolò Amati (1596–1684), Antonio Stradivari (1644–1737), and Giuseppe Bartolomeo Guarneri "del Gesù" (1698–1744), thus making the age that of great Italian string music.

The ensemble sonatas of the Venetian Giovanni Gabrieli provided soloistic opportunities from time to time, as did the chamber music of his student, the organist Giovanni Valentini, whose 1639 sonata, for example, for violin, cornettino, bassoon, and trombone permitted a different instrument to predominate in each movement. Valentini, like many Italians, moved north and spent much of his time in Graz and Vienna. Biagio Marini, a Brescian who spent many years in Düsseldorf, was perhaps the first professional violin virtuoso among composers and wrote one of the first sonatas with double stops and *scordatura* (the deliberate retuning of the instrument to make it easier to play chords). His contemporary Carlo Farina, who, like Marini, belonged to the Mantuan violin school under Claudio Monteverdi, wrote works requiring the violinist to play fairly high in the range of his instrument as well as on the G-string, the lowest string, which was rarely used in the early days of the violin, and *sul ponticello* (on the bridge). The violinist had to play *col legno* (with the wood of the bow) and produce double stops, pizzicati, tremolos, and glissandi. Farina, noted for his stunts and for his programmatic ideas, headed north to Germany where he worked with a student of Giovanni Gabrieli, Heinrich Schütz, in Dresden. Soloists, then, appeared early in the seventeenth century in Italy and migrated to Germany. Early on, they had developed the virtuoso devices and techniques with which Paganini would make his name two centuries later.

The presence of Maurizio Cazzati, his pupil Giovanni Battista Vitali, the Accademia dei Filarmonici, and two publishers helped make Bologna a major center; but an important jewel in its crown must have been the musical chapel of the church of San Petronio. Its small but fine orchestra permitted Cazzati in 1665 to introduce ensemble "sonatas" that included trumpets. The Bolognese composers spun off a literature of such works well into the eighteenth century. When large celebrations were scheduled, the chapel added extra musicians of probably inferior abilities. With that practical consideration, composers for the chapel would write works in which relatively easy material could be performed by the entire instrumental body (the tutti, or ripieno) and virtuosic passages were reserved for the resident experts, thereby foreshadowing the concertino of the concerto grosso.

24

In the hands of such composers as Giovanni Legrenzi, Alessandro Stradella, Torelli, Arcangelo Corelli, and his students Francesco Geminiani and Pietro Locatelli, instrumental forms like the sonata, concerto, concerto grosso, concertino, and sinfonia developed. Terminological difficulties abound as one confronts these words. Not only did the same terms mean different things to different composers, but their meanings actually overlapped.

Corelli's students expanded upon the teachings of their master and broadcast them to the world. Geminiani took the concerto grosso to England where he elaborated its contrapuntal texture and ornaments. Locatelli, in Holland, established a rich surface against which the violin solo could stand out. Georg Muffat, who may have studied with Corelli, took the form back to Salzburg and Passau.

Torelli may have sketched the first solo concerto, but Antonio Vivaldi, a formidable violinist by all reports, expanded the solo passages and their Torellian pyrotechnics whether he was writing for violin, cello, flute, or bassoon. The early violin concerto, created by professional composer-violinists primarily for their own use—though some violinists championed the works of other composers—reached its peak in Italy with the eighteenth-century Paduan virtuoso and theorist Giuseppe Tartini, who casually performed double stops, double trills with any finger, and dizzyingly high passages without apparent effort.

Of the virtuoso-composers who emulated Tartini there were many, not the least of whom were Pietro Nardini, his student, and Gaetano Pugnani, an important link in the Corelli-Somis-Pugnani-Viotti chain.

In Italy, each time virtuosic developments pushed toward acrobatics, a conservative composer (Corelli, Tartini, Pugnani, Viotti) would remind the gymnasts that the violin was meant to sing. Rossini, in 1817, objected to certain vocal practices of his time: "the warblings, wild leaps and jumps, trills, misuse of semitones, notes all tangled up. . . . Whereas in better times the performers tried to make their instruments sing, our singers now try to make their voices play."

Owing to the sophisticated polyphonic virtuosity already possible on the lute and the bass member of the viola da gamba family, in Spain, England, and North Germany the violin did not become popular until the end of the seventeenth century. The arrival in London of Thomas Baltzar from Lübeck and of the Italian Nicola Matteis in

XLVI *Tiorba*

In these eighteenth-century engravings by Arnold van Westerhout, the lute is incorrectly identified as a theorbo, the cello as a viola. The next four plates, from the same source (Filippo Bonanni's Gabinetto Armonico, *1723), depict a French horn, trumpet, violin, and a much-simplified clavicytherium.*

LVI *Viola*

1672 finally helped popularize the violin there. Bruce Bellingham quotes Anthony Wood, who recorded the first performance of Baltzar in Oxford on 24 July 1658. Wood, himself an amateur gambist and not particularly enthusiastic about the violin, saw Baltzar "run up his fingers to the end of the finger board . . . and run them back insensibly, and all with alacrity and in very good tune. . . ." In describing Baltzar's second performance there a few days later, Wood writes, "Wilson thereupon, the public professor, (the greatest judg of musick that ever was) did, after his humoursome way, stoop downe to Baltzar's feet, to see whether he had a huff on, that is to say to see whether he was a devill or not, because he acted beyond the parts of man."

26

In France the violin had been popular only for ballet. Lully may have been a violin virtuoso, but after his youth he focused his interests elsewhere. The first great exponent of the violin in France was Jean-Marie Leclair, a student of the Italian Giovanni Battista Somis, himself a pupil of Corelli and a teacher of Pugnani. Leclair, a pre-Classical composer, brought the early violin concerto to its apogee in France.

Germany produced virtuoso-composers like Nikolaus Adam Strungk, whose double-stops astounded Corelli; Johann Heinrich Schmelzer, who in 1660 was characterized as the celebrated and "nearly finest *violisten* in all Europe"; Johann Jakob Walther, whose solo sonatas were thesauri of virtuosic devices (except for *scordatura*, for which he had contempt); Johann Paul Westhoff, whose 1682 suite for violin alone was one of the two earliest and most important predecessors of Bach's unaccompanied music, particularly the Chaconne; and, of course, the outstanding virtuoso violinist and composer in seventeenth-century Germany and Austria, Heinrich von Biber, in the service of the Archbishop of Salzburg. Biber's Passacaglia, the sixteenth Rosary or *Mystery* Sonata (ca. 1675) was the other important predecessor of Bach's Chaconne.

The development of a high level of virtuosity on the viola da gamba retarded acceptance of the cello just as it had the violin, but for a longer time. The *Ricercari* (1689) of the Bolognese Domenico Gabrieli is probably the earliest example of a work for solo cello. Gabrieli's student Giuseppe Jacchini, the best cellist of his era, published some cello sonatas the same year and wrote the first cello concerto in 1701.

The first cello soloist of European fame, Franciscello (Francesco Alborea), helped put the viola da gamba *hors de combat*. Cello sonatas and concerti proliferated in his wake. Another performer of Italian provenance, Batistin (Jean-Baptiste Stuck, born of German parents in Livorno or Florence), introduced the cello to the Paris Opéra about 1702. The Valenciennois Martin Berteau was the first French cello virtuoso of European standing. A gambist by training, he switched instruments after hearing Franciscello and won over the French public when he played the cello at the *Concerts spirituels* in 1739. Many then followed in his footsteps; the most important were the Duport brothers, Jean-Pierre and Jean-Louis, the latter a student of the former, who had likewise been inspired by Franciscello. Although Mozart and Beethoven wrote for Jean-Pierre, his younger

27

XVII *Corno Raddoppiato*

IV *Tromba doppia*

brother founded the French school of cello playing, doing for the cello what Casals would do a century later: rethink the whole problem of fingering and bowing technique.

From Lucca came Luigi Boccherini, who played notes much higher on the cello than anyone else until a century later. About 1766 in Florence, he reputedly formed the first established string quartet with his friend Filippo Manfredi (a pupil of Nardini and Tartini), Nardini himself, and Giovanni Giuseppe Cambini (who may have played viola although he was a violin pupil of Manfredi and Nardini).

The cello, like the violin, made its way much more slowly in Germany than elsewhere. In Cöthen, Prince Leopold had taken on many members of the Berlin Hofkapelle orchestra which had been dissolved

28

on the death of Friedrich I in February 1713. Bach had gone to Cöthen to serve as *Kapellmeister* of Prince Leopold's court orchestra from 1717 to 1723. Its instrumentalists included Christian Bernhard Linigke, an outstanding cellist for whom Bach may have written the unaccompanied cello suites. After Bach, composers continued to write works for cello, but interest in unaccompanied cello works disappeared until Casals revived Bach's suites; finally, in 1914 and 1915 respectively, Max Reger and Zoltán Kodály wrote pieces for unaccompanied cello.

The organ and harpsichord had long genealogical lines of virtuosi. Italy contributed early examples of excellence with Frescobaldi and Claudio Merulo in the sixteenth century. The Netherlands contributed Jan Pieterszoon Sweelinck, and England contributed John Bull,

LXVII   *Violino*

XLIV   *Cembalo Verticale*

among others. Brilliant virtuosic effects established the keyboards in north and central Germany in the late seventeenth and eighteenth centuries. One of the foremost of keyboard virtuosi was Johann Sebastian Bach. A solid citizen and hardly the demonic individual that the nineteenth-century audience was to perceive in its own virtuosi, Bach won musical duels partly because he played devilishly fast. He wrote the Six Brandenburg Concerti for the forces at Cöthen and probably wrote the Fifth planning his own performance at the keyboard of the instrument he himself had chosen for Leopold. In the Fifth Concerto, solo flute and violin form the concertino group. Bach labeled the harpsichord part "concertato." The instrument, part of the continuo and ripieno, initially shuttles back and forth in the first movement between orchestral and solo roles but gradually intrudes into the concertino and eventually prevails over its other two members in a written-out cadenza so intensively developed—a second version is more "sober"—and extended in time that the almost unbearable unresolved tension, created by frustrating the expectation of the recurrence of the tutti's refrain—as the reader of this sentence must be frustrated awaiting its full stop—in a form dependent upon the timbral and functional alternation of concertino episodes and orchestral ritornello, stretches the form to its limits and almost destroys it (and in so doing sets the stage for a new form, the solo keyboard concerto).

Mozart, the first great piano virtuoso, wrote his piano concerti for his own use. Ironically, he was the last great composer to focus on the concerto as the major part of his output. Production of a certain kind of music often results from a specific need: Mozart depended on concerti for his living, whereas Haydn, not a traveling virtuoso, needed, and therefore wrote, few of them. As salon performances and then solo recitals became increasingly popular, the solo sonata took a leading position in the output of composer-performers, hence one reason for the importance of sonatas in Beethoven's oeuvre.

Mozart probably destined his violin concerti for Gaetano Brunetti, a great virtuoso, composer, and close family friend; Ignaz Leutgeb, hornist, violinist, composer, cheesemonger, and close musical friend of longest standing, was recipient of all the horn concertos, despite Mozart's acquaintance with the greatest horn virtuosi of the time, the Bohemian Giovanni Punto (b. Jan Václav Stich—an Italian name must have been synonymous with musicality) and Franz Anton Rösler (Rosetti). Anton Stadler, clarinetist, fellow Mason, and friend, was likewise closely connected with Mozart's clarinet compositions. Carl Maria von Weber and Felix Mendelssohn produced works for the German clarinet virtuoso Heinrich Joseph Bärmann. With increasing regularity, composers began to write for specific performers other than themselves.

Clearly, then, performers had come upon the scene who, though they may have composed, were primarily transmitters of music written by other musicians who were primarily composers. Considering the damage some performers occasionally do to composers' works, one is tempted to damn the species, but that would be a mistake. In the eighteenth century, men like Giuseppe Sammartini and Alessandro Besozzi popularized the oboe, while others, like Anton Joseph Hampel, experimented on the horn. Jean-Joseph Rodolphe and Spandau, respectively, introduced the hand horn to Paris in 1765 and to London in 1773. With regard to the flute, in the nineteenth century Charles Nicholson and Theobald Böhm would, in the case of the former, influence the aesthetics of tone and, in that of the latter, the actual mechanics of performance.

Performers can also act as propagandists. Ignaz Schuppanzigh was a violinist, violist, conductor, and close friend of Beethoven. As first violin in a quartet that regularly played for Prince Lichnowsky and as founder in 1808 of Prince Razumovsky's private quartet, Schuppanzigh helped shape the performing traditions of Beethoven's as well as Haydn's and Mozart's quartets.

Beethoven, especially in his fourth and fifth piano concerti and his violin concerto, assimilated the advanced techniques of the violinists Pierre Gaviniès and Giovanni Battista Viotti, as well as the keyboard virtuosity of Nicholas-Joseph Hüllmandel and Daniel Steibelt. From these influences would flow the piano concertos of J.L. Dussek, Field, Moscheles, Kalkbrenner, Herz, Weber, Chopin, Mendelssohn, Liszt, Brahms, Lalo, Saint-Saëns, Anton Rubinstein, Tchaikovsky, and Reger and the violin concertos of Spohr, Bruch, Mendelssohn, Brahms, Tchaikovsky, Dvořák, and Pfitzner.

The case of Domenico Dragonetti dramatically illustrates the progressive role virtuosi can play. When in the spring of 1799 he performed Beethoven's Sonata for Piano with Cello Obbligato, op. 5 (written for Pierre Duport) on his double-bass viol with Beethoven at the keyboard, Dragonetti showed Beethoven what the instrument could do. This resulted in far more difficult bass parts in Beethoven's orchestral works (the trio of the Scherzo in the Fifth Symphony is a classic example). Indeed, yesterday's virtuosi have set the standard for today's orchestral player.

As we move closer to our time and as instrumental music becomes more idiomatic, so too differentiation and then specialization of composer and performer take place, and eventually the tension between the two, though not new, becomes exacerbated.

During the time of E.T.A. Hoffmann (1776–1822), the artist had been the idol of society. But he degenerated to the level of superstar and, after the 1830s affected various bohemianisms. That period appears to be the locus of all lunacy, yet the sense of déjà vu with regard to so many elements in the discussion of virtuosity (the attitudes for and against it, the techniques developed and their positive or negative values, the dress code, servants, temperament, artist's social role, foreignness, amatory pursuits, financial embarrassments, and so forth) is confirmed by accounts throughout history and across the globe.

Contradiction is a hallmark of the nineteenth century. The performer no longer was expected to act as agent for the composer; rather, as an individual he had to rework the composition in his own soul, thereby becoming a re-creator. The Romantic aesthetic idealized the intimate, subjective, dreamlike, and exalted states. But instead of performing in an appropriately small salon for a discriminating minority of connoisseurs, the newly sensitized *artiste* found himself in relatively large halls (though small by our standards) facing large audiences whose taste was questionable and whose musical literacy was negligible.

Most concerts still were more or less private and were given for about three or four hundred people, though a special event might have been arranged for as many as 800. The crowd of 1,500 at Thalberg's concert at the Théâtre Italien was almost unheard of. Yet Liszt, on his first appearance at St. Petersburg, drew 3,000.

Introspection, small alterations of ideas, gentle formal surprises, nuanced dynamics, intricately reasoned musical arguments, all the stuff of solo and chamber music, had to be blasted to the rafters; subtlety had to be engrossed. Pierre Rode attacked the problem with showpieces called *quatuors brillants*. Even the conservative Ludwig Spohr, who tried to remain true to the eighteenth-century conception of chamber music, wrote "solo quartets," thinly disguised chamber concertos for solo violin and string trio. The piano, poetically perfect for the intimate idea, became increasingly mechanically solid and more powerful, able to do battle with the orchestra, a fact that did not go unnoticed by either composer or performer, who attempted to make the piano sound like one.

Yet the concerto began to fade in importance. It had been part of a tradition of made-to-order music for a performer, the composer, who had to sell himself. The symphony had already dominated the end of the eighteenth century: Beethoven, Schubert, Weber, Mendelssohn, Chopin, and Liszt, all pianists, did most of their important work in genres other than the concerto, because large orchestras required large halls and that cost money. The nineteenth century was a time of supposedly disinterested inspiration and self-expression: small solo pieces could be performed in salons and, where necessary, could also serve for self-display.

From that time (and, in truth, from well before it also), the number of performers is staggering who were important both on the stages of the world and to the history of virtuosity and the development of instruments, musical forms, and taste. They swarmed across Europe and, from about 1848, to the Western Hemisphere. "Virtuoso" implied *extraordinary* skill, but once again the truths of relativism strike a blow against clear definition: extraordinary skill has been common. Indicative of transient fame is the ringing irony of glowing epithets once enthusiastically employed to describe the (now all but forgotten) "Paganini of the double bass" (Dragonetti) or the "French Mozart" (Devienne).

How could one not mention the Viennese pianist Sigismond Thalberg, whose own music eclipsed Chopin's in his day and whom Liszt described as "the only artist who can play the violin on the keyboard"? But there are many others, truly important, about whom similar things were said, who because of their espousal of unpopular but ultimately important causes should be mentioned but will not be because these brief notes would degenerate into a catalog.

Curiously, Frédéric Chopin is really not a part of this story; he was a composer who happened to perform, a master of his instrument who rarely played for the masses, who restricted his performances to the salons of the elite, and who lived in relative seclusion.

The figures who tower over all the others are the demoniacal Italian violinist Niccolò Paganini (1782–1840) and, eventually, the young Hungarian pianist Franz Liszt (1811–86). The public went berserk over Paganini and invented myths to explain his way with the fiddle. In the age of the Brothers Grimm, Weber's Evil One, Ber-

33

lioz's "Witches' Sabbath," Schubert's *Doppelgänger,* Goethe's *Faust,* and Mesmer's fluid magnetism, it was easy to believe that this spindly limbed man with hyperextended, bony fingers, a high wide forehead, large ears, a toothless mouth resembling Voltaire's, and long hair on a large head set on a thin neck, might very well have sold his soul to the devil to play like him. His controversial personality and the rumors of his life contributed to the mystery: gay, melancholy, angry, jovial, generous, witty, avaricious, wealthy, poor, a doting father, gambler, womanizer. . . . Toward the end, he talked little, that is true; aphonic, he died of laryngial tuberculosis, which disease may account for his unsociability and for the closed windows of his carriage while he traveled, enveloped in furs, in 68° weather.

We do know certain things about him; he had great press and knew how to use it. Alfred de Vigny, in his First Parisian Letter in *L'Avenir* of 3 April 1831, summed up the hysterical build-up in the journals prior to Paganini's arrival in Paris: "They created for him his small fears, his secrets, his jail terms, and his homicide; because a certain little scent of crime and despair is always necessary for us here in order to be well received in the world. He is pallid, ravaged, emaciated: he lacks nothing."

Many knowledgeable musicians spoke well of him. "I have wept only three times in my life," wrote Rossini, "the first time when my earliest opera failed, the second time when, on a boating party, a truffled turkey fell into the water, and the third time when I first heard Paganini." Though he was not beyond a Barnumesque caper of cutting three strings with a pair of scissors and then playing on one string or, on occasion, substituting a cane for the bow, he nevertheless was admired for his musicianship by his friend Mendelssohn, and by Schubert, Berlioz, and Chopin. Fakers don't collect admirers like that.

On the surface, Paganini incarnated E.T.A. Hoffmann's infernal violinist, yet he added little to the kinds of special techniques that violinists had been using for many years (harmonics, multiple stops, left-hand pizzicati, tremolos, *col legno, sul ponticello,* and *scordatura*). He played without music, and the orchestra members said that what he played at the concerts was not what they had heard at the rehearsal; like many virtuosi, he was secretive about his techniques and tricks.

He apparently improvised effortlessly, brilliantly, and movingly, using the devices abundantly with demonic skill, precision, beauty, power, control, passion, and intense energy—in a word, transcen-

Niccolò Paganini—Satan's tool? Oil, ca. 1830, Georg Friedrich Kersting; Staatliche Gemäldegalerie, Dresden

dentally. Perhaps just a talented composer with a gift for melody, harmonic richness, instrumental effects, and an elegant sense of form, Paganini was probably the world's best improviser; the notes that have come down to us, pale indeed in light of the fuss made over him and indicating "a lean and precise classicism" (in the words of Abraham Veinus), probably have little if any relation to what he actually played. After all, Schubert told a friend, "Such a fellow will never come again."

Paganini exerted little influence as a teacher, the most noteworthy lines extending from his student Camillo Sivori to Rosario Scalero, whose students are the composers Barber, Menotti, and Foss, and to Zino Francescatti via his father. Almost all French violinists, for example, can be traced back to Viotti, but Paganini's fame, though deserved, eclipsed the contributions of other violinists.

The French violin school, in fact, is based on the work of three others: Pierre Rode and Pierre Baillot, students of Viotti, and Rodolphe Kreutzer, a student of Anton Stamitz but who modeled himself after Viotti. Tracing a lineage devolving from teacher to student, we note:

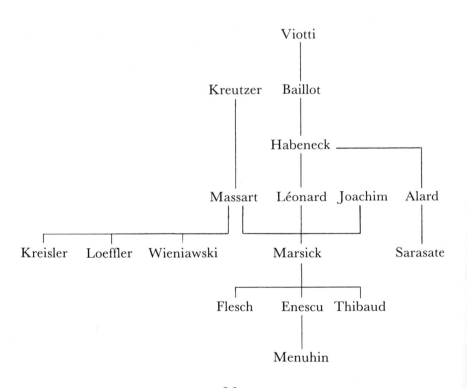

36

Following a slightly different line: Viotti-Rode-Böhm-Hellmesberger-Enescu. Now note the next pedigree:

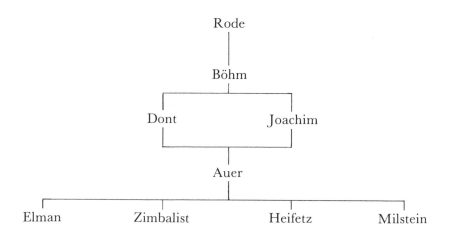

Thus the so-called Russian school stems from Austrian and French roots. In the Kreutzer line, the crucial student is Lambert-Joseph Massart, for it is he who taught Marsick, Kreisler, Loeffler (who also studied with Léonard and Joachim), and Wieniawski.

A number of the early members of the French school promoted the music of Beethoven. François Habeneck, who held the role of violin soloist at the Opéra when Kreutzer became conductor and was active in the renewed *Concerts spirituels* from 1805, founded the Société des Concerts du Conservatoire de Paris in 1828, which often featured the works of Beethoven. Habeneck's teacher, Baillot, formed the first professional quartet in Paris in 1814; its violist, the devoted Beethovenian, Chrétien Urhan, the well-known, highly respected virtuoso for whom Meyerbeer would write the viola solo in *Les Huguenots,* played the première of Berlioz's *Harold in Italy,* written for Paganini but turned down by him because it was not virtuosic enough.

Still, one cannot write off Paganini's influence. Charles-Auguste de Bériot antedates and postdates Paganini. Though a pupil of Viotti and Robberechts, he was one of the first to assimilate Paganini's developments into his own writing and teaching. De Bériot founded the tasteful and elegant Franco-Belgian school. His most famous pupil was Henri Vieuxtemps. The Pole Henri Wieniawski, a pupil of Massart and one of the most famous violinists of the century, taught briefly at Brussels; his energetic bravura and warm, sentimental nationalism enriched his virtuosity.

Eugène Ysaÿe (1858–1931) is one of the last in the centuries-old tradition of virtuosi with schooling and creativity sufficient to venture into composing. A pupil of Massart, Wieniawski, and Vieuxtemps, he was almost alone in first performing the music of Debussy, Franck, and Lekeu. In addition to teaching Jacques Thibaud, perhaps the greatest of French violinists, Ysaÿe taught Louis Persinger and Naoum Blinder, both of whom taught Isaac Stern. Persinger, who also studied with Thibaud, taught Menuhin and Ruggiero Ricci, Ysaÿe convinced William Primrose to take up the viola.

By the beginning of the nineteenth century few performers were complete musicians. Paraphrases or variations of the most popular hits from the latest operas, dazzling concerti, and meritricious *études brillantes* were designed to show off the technique and personality of performers like Daniel Steibelt, Friedrich Kalkbrenner, Ignaz Moscheles, and Henri Herz. The piano, considered to be almost a domestic diversion, had not quite established its credentials as an instrument for serious study. Cherubini had reduced the number of piano students at Paris's Conservatoire in 1822; only fifteen years later did he first hear Beethoven's piano sonatas. But by the late 1820s in Paris, and in the rest of Europe in the thirties and forties, competition boomed among piano makers. After 1836, the new piano actions, new methods of stringing, and the stronger body coincided to make a powerful, resonant, agile, and brilliant instrument. Pianists lent their names to, or joined the thriving businesses of, the Clementis, Pleyels, and Erards. The time was ripe. Paganini had set the stage with some compositional models that would answer the performer's needs. But his works were more than formal models: they announced a new aesthetic.

Paganini's Twenty-four Caprices were études; their shortness helped shape the taste for terse character pieces as well as for the many sets of études and préludes that the century produced. Schumann, Brahms, Rachmaninoff, Busoni, Tommasini, Blacher, Lutoslawski, and Liszt are among the many composers who tran-

38

scribed Paganini's works or used them as bases for sets of variations.

In 1832 Liszt, after hearing Paganini play, wrote a *Grande Fantaisie de bravoure sur la Clochette* (i.e., "La Campanella") from the rondo of Paganini's Concerto No. 2 in B minor, op. 7. In 1838 he followed with six *Etudes d'exécution transcendante d'après Paganini* (the third is "La Campanella") but on a smaller scale. The other five of the set are transcriptions of Paganini's caprices for solo violin, published about 1830. In 1851 Liszt published a simplified version. Busoni eventually published his own version of the entire set of twenty-four caprices; thus they contain the names of three of the greatest virtuosi in history. It was not only the tunes that interested all these composers; it was Paganini's idea of a virtuosity that expands musical expressivity at the same time that it is diabolically exciting. Liszt sensed this as a young man, shortly after hearing Paganini play.

Handsome and gifted, Liszt was younger still (eleven years old) when he came to Vienna to study with Czerny. Within a year, he had performed at least two well-received concerts, had improvised for Beethoven in private, and had overcome several of Beethoven's prejudices, including his dislike of child prodigies. Having been kissed by Beethoven, Liszt felt himself consecrated for a life in music.

A seriousness of purpose (perhaps more than the desire to astound) informed Liszt's thought, his composition, his arrangements, and his programming from the start. Today, we disapprove of tampering with a composer's work, but aesthetic attitudes were different then. Liszt performed the Beethoven symphonies and Schubert songs in transcription, as well as opera scenes and fantasies, musical travelogues, works inspired by paintings and literature; and paraphrases and transcriptions. It was his way to get these works as well as Bach's organ works and Wagner's music dramas into homes or onto a stage. It was a form of music education. (Incidentally, the process of making transcriptions of opera arias was not very different from that of the keyboard intablatures and instrumental *canzonas* of the Renaissance period.)

Liszt started his ascension in Paris and worked east. In Vienna, Hanslick quipped, "The ladies lost their hearts and the critics their heads." The hysteria surrounding Liszt was akin to that surrounding Frank Sinatra, Elvis Presley, and the Beatles a century later. In Pesth, 20,000 people marched in a torch-light parade toward his residence there. Women threw themselves on their knees and tried to kiss his fingertips. Like their plectra-snatching Greek sisters, they col-

Liszt in concert: "The ladies lost their hearts and the critics their heads." Frontispiece, Berlin, wie es ist und—trinkts, *vol. 14, Adam Brennglas, Leipzig, 1842*

lected the dregs of his tea or his cigar butts and put them in vials which they wore next to their bosoms.

In disgust, Liszt, who had been first to turn the piano sideways so that the audience could see his profile, cut short his virtuoso career and gave his final recital in Russia in 1847. Except for a brief time, he no longer played piano solos in his own concerts. Instead, he returned to Weimar to compose, conduct, and teach.

Liszt raised piano technique to a level unknown before him. In the popularization of music history, two composers of the same period are often paired as if they were twins; only with familiarity do we realize that those composers often stand poles apart, as do Bach and Handel or Haydn and Mozart. So it is with Chopin and Liszt. It has been said that Chopin made the piano sound like a piano; Liszt made it sound like an orchestra. They spun off two distinct schools of piano playing: from Liszt devolved Hans von Bülow, Tausig, Anton Rubinstein, Saint-Saëns, d'Albert, and Busoni. From Chopin came Paderewski, Pugno, Pachmann, and Cortot.

Clearly, not everyone was frivolous before 1848. A small conservative underground of professional and amateur musicians, private societies, and the semi-private and strictly conservative Société des Concerts du Conservatoire performed Bach, Handel, Haydn, Mozart, and Beethoven. The state of music improved a little at the end of the 1840s when the foundation of the Société Alard-Franchomme spurred other chamber-music and Beethoven societies to form. (Jean-Delphin Alard, a student of the Beethovenian Habeneck, succeeded Baillot as teacher of violin at the Conservatoire; Auguste-Joseph Franchomme, an intimate of Chopin, had earlier performed chamber music in Paris with Charles Hallé, founder of the Hallé Orchestra in Manchester, England.)

Inexpensive Sunday afternoon concerts, the *Concerts populaires* founded by Pasdeloup in 1860, introduced the public to Beethoven, Mendelssohn, and Schumann. But frivolity on the one hand and conservatism on the other did not nourish a healthy atmosphere for young composers. French music did not become vital again until the Franco-Prussian war and the Commune, when the Société Nationale de Musique was founded in 1871 to re-establish an "Ars Gallica"; from the SNM began to flow much new chamber music and a spirit that marked the renaissance of French music.

Meanwhile, in the first half of the century, in German-speaking cities like Vienna and Leipzig sober recitals were given in which the musical text no longer served solely as a means for a performer to show off; now performers sought to illuminate and interpret the text.

Robert Schumann stigmatized as Philistines showy performers like Thalberg, Herz, and Czerny and the composers of opera fantasies, galops, polkas, and facile variations with French titles, and he called to arms his *Davidsbündler* to meet them in battle. But his generals, Clara (née Wieck) Schumann, who branded Liszt's followers as "pounders," the pianist, conductor, composer, editor, and writer Hans von Bülow and the great violinist Joseph Joachim, composer and close friend of Brahms (whom he introduced to the Schumanns), wielded more than sling shots as they performed the works of

Beethoven, Chopin, Schubert, Schumann, Mendelssohn, and Brahms. Clara, a composer in her own right and an important pianist, had been one of the first persons who dared play Beethoven's sonatas to a public concert audience. Hanslick, Wagner's Beckmesser, praised her for playing only Beethoven sonatas on a recital in 1837 and for not being one of those performers who wrote sonatas as vehicles for their own display.

The century's involvement with history had finally impinged upon the consciousness of soloists, for while emotional displays were part of the Romantic spirit—whatever that may mean (and it means many contradictory things)—so was an interest in the past; "roman" refers to the Romanesque period, and it was characteristic of the time in which the discipline of musicology was born to scour the past for its determinants and to resuscitate its folk tales and racial legends in a search for "pure" origins, in short, getting to the roots of what was unfortunately to develop via Gobineau, Wagner, and others into Nazism.

Because of the Revolution of 1848, many musicians—most of the pianists were not French anyway—fled the insecurities of the Second Republic for England or America. Charles Hallé went to London where he proposed performing a solo sonata at a select morning chamber music series. Although its manager resisted on grounds of unsuitability and lack of precedence—*plus ça change, plus c'est la même chose*—he finally gave in. Hallé successfully made his point with Beethoven's opus 31 no. 3 and gave London a new precedent.

In the United States performers like Henri Herz and Jenny Lind began to swarm over the continent from about 1846. Boston's Mendelssohn and Quintette Club, organized in 1849, gave what are probably the first good performances of chamber music here. Many halls were built, and many concerts (or *Grandes Soirées musicales*) called for pianists, but solo recitals did not become common until after 1870. Pianists initially brought their European pianos with them but soon changed to American products.

Although the regular concert-goer might hear a Beethoven concerto or sonata every now and then—the "Waldstein" Sonata was first heard in the spring of 1859 during the season when the name Steinway made its first appearance at a chamber concert in New York—the public would more likely encounter the "Prayer" from Rossini's *Otello,* "executed with the left hand alone."

The New Orleans pianist Louis-Moreau Gottschalk, who had

42

Paris showroom of the Becker piano firm. L'Illustration, *1878*

introduced Creole, Afro-Hispanic, and other American tunes and ideas to Europe, returned to the United States in 1853 and pursued a successful career until he was stricken with yellow fever on tour in Rio de Janeiro. Thalberg, the most celebrated, able, and effective concert pianist to tour during the 1850s, included both "classics" and American tunes in his repertory.

Steinway built its own hall in New York in 1866, associated itself in 1872 with the New York orchestra of the immensely influential conductor Theodore Thomas, and just as the European piano firms Pleyel, Broadwood, and Erard had sponsored performers, so Steinway underwrote Anton Rubinstein's tour of 1872. (Arthur Loesser, in *Men, Women, and Pianos,* records a quip of the time: "'Instead of saying "Herr Wischer uses the Hammerschlag piano," the announcement ought to read "The Hammerschlag Piano Co. uses Herr Wischer."''''' Ninety pages of letters of endorsement in facsimile and in translation, complete with photographs of their authors—men like Liszt, Berlioz, and Wagner—appear in a hardcover Steinway publication of 1922, *Portraits of Musical Celebrities—A Book of Notable Testimonials.*) Rubinstein played 215 concerts in 239 days, performing in cities as far apart as New York, Montreal, Toronto, New Orleans, and Central City, Colorado. The music of Bach, Beethoven, Chopin, Schumann, and Rubinstein figured in his programs; at times he gave joint recitals with Wieniawski.

Chickering sponsored von Bülow, who opened in Boston with the American premiere of Tchaikovsky's B-flat minor piano concerto. In New York von Bülow did an all-Beethoven program with Leopold Damrosch's orchestra. In 1889 Knabe underwrote his tour. Then in 1891 Steinway signed Ignace Paderewski, who captured the American imagination as no other artist had ever done.

By the end of the century tastes were changing in Europe and America. Programming became more austere, execution less eccentric, and the kind of naive tricks that Barnum would have loved began to recede into history. In 1879 Édouard Lalo suggested to the extraordinary Pablo de Sarasate, whose grace, beautiful tone, impeccable intonation, and technical perfection were legendary, that he perform Brahms's Violin Concerto. It was still not outlandish for the violinist, who had the concerto's slow movement in mind, to retort, "Do you think me so devoid of taste that I would stand there in front of the orchestra, violin in hand, but like a listener, while the oboe plays the only melody in the entire work?" Sarasate seemed to be echoing Paganini's attitude about Berlioz's *Harold in Italy*, but it was not many years later when a French audience hissed a performance by Paderewski of Beethoven's G-major concerto, not because of the pianist's interpretation but because he used a "virtuoso vehicle."

The clarinetist Richard Mühlfeld exemplified a more serious approach to one's instrument: his performance at Meiningen's Castle in 1891 inspired Brahms to come out of retirement and write four works for the clarinet, including the great quintet. Bravura was still to the fore, but just as Brahms could coexist with Liszt or Wagner, so Joachim or Mühlfeld might coexist with Pachmann.

The antics of few virtuosi could rival those of the often-married Vladimir de Pachmann. Late in his career, he would come out on stage, fuss with the height of his piano bench, leave the stage, return with a phone book, sit on it, fuss some more, than rip out one page and, satisfied, commence playing. He grimaced if he did not like the way he played; if he did like his performance, he was the first to yell "Bravo!" At times he would crawl underneath the piano and then explain to the audience that he was looking for all the notes he had dropped. Worse, he inserted arpeggios here and there and added chords at the end. (Wilhelm Backhaus, a far more serious performer, would simply come out on stage, sit down, play some arpeggios, and then cadence directly into the first notes of the programmed work.) Although the brilliant American critic James Huneker occasionally found Pachmann's performances poetic and sensitive, he called him "the original Chopinzee."

Dignified soloists also entertained the public (for example, Paderewski; Ysaÿe, who performed with Anton Rubinstein and knew Franck and d'Indy; and Raoul Pugno, who performed in duo recitals with Ysaÿe in 1904).

As the bourgeoisie had become more sophisticated, groups of educated music lovers in Germany became more powerful and, after 1871, exported their German ideas through their émigrés. (America's basic musical attitudes have remained Germanic despite several subsequent "injections" of French and American blood and numerous American aesthetic revolutions.)

The Russian pianist and composer Anton Rubinstein had an immense impact on music everywhere. In 1873 he still had doubts about performing more than one Beethoven sonata per program, but on 25 and 29 May 1876 in London, he very successfully performed programs in which almost everything he played was from 20 to 150 years old. In 1878, however, von Bülow was censured in London for playing an all-Beethoven recital; worse, for choosing the last five sonatas at that; and worse still, for doing them all from memory. Yet by 1861 complete cycles of the thirty-two sonatas had been performed and, not long after, from memory, by Charles Hallé in London, (1861) and by Carl Wolfsohn in Philadelphia and New York (1863). (Consistency has never been the critics's strong suit.) The favorites then were those favored today. In London in 1883 a performance of Beethoven's "Kreutzer" Sonata by Clara Schumann and Joseph Joachim was advertised as being the forty-eighth "at these concerts."

That good taste was winning over bad seems laudable on the surface, but an insidious element insinuated itself between 1850 and 1890: almost all the composers in Rubinstein's programs were dead.

Joseph Joachim and Clara Schumann in a chamber music concert. Drawing, 1854, Adolph von Menzel; Robert Shumann Haus, Zwickau

The museum nature of concert life was becoming enshrined. In 1885/ 86 Rubinstein gave a seven-concert series of "historical" programs throughout Europe, performing music from the mid-sixteenth through the mid-nineteenth centuries. (His own concerti were the first Russian concerti to make a stir in the West.)

Concerts averaged two hours or more. Some were much longer and might include Beethoven's op. 106 (a favorite), Weber's op. 39, Brahms's op. 5, and Liszt's B-minor Sonata. Rubinstein once played the entire B-minor Sonata of Chopin as his first encore. Other works were introduced piecemeal: von Bülow gave the première of the first movement of Brahms's op. 1 in 1854; the same year, Clara Schumann played only the second and third movements of the op. 5. Individual movements became so popular that they were often played alone.

Programs might announce works without giving the composer's name or announce generic titles (Gigue or Nocturne or Sonata) without further identification. Foreignness must have lent a certain *je ne sais quoi* to a program. On an English program can be read the following: "Beethoven, *Marcia alla Turca* (Des 'Ruines d'Athènes')," titles in two languages neither of which could be read by either audience or composer, a macaronic announcing what appears to be an Italian march in Turkish (or Janissary) style from a French play about Greece. Did the English audience ever guess that the music was to a German play, *Die Ruinen von Athen* by the important playwright August von Kotzebue? The program identified the Russian pianist as *Herr* Rubinstein.

Thus, music had moved out of private clubs into public halls whose management assisted in the alchemy that transmogrified them into temples. (The religious ritual is still extant at Bayreuth.) Taste had shifted from the glib, shallow modish to the pernicious and sacrosanct necromantic, and had deleteriously established that ostentatious intellectual and aesthetic pose characterized by Pound as *Kulchur*. And the soloist, who in earlier times had been a juggler, tambourine salesman, and salon dandy, metamorphosed into High Priest.

The virtuosi gathered in this collection, whose lives and work are treated in Richard Freed's commentary elsewhere in this book, represent the next and ensuing generations. It is not possible to make wholesale generalizations about them and their colleagues: some composed, some hid their light under a bushel, some were interested in the music of their time, some became curators of the musical museum, and some seemed interested only in technical mastery. Nor did all of them play the instruments associated with the nineteenth-century stage. Very much in a class by himself, Andrés Segovia made the classical guitar once again a serious concert instrument. He has had works written for it by Castelnuovo-Tedesco, Manuel Ponce, Joaquín Turina, and Albert Roussel.

The eighteenth century had new instruments like Franklin's glass harmonica and a virtuoso, Marianne Kirchgässner, to commission works for it. The saxophone was an old instrument before it truly hit its solo stride in the twentieth century. Although it was used as early as 1844 (about the time Adolphe Sax took out patents on it) by Jean Georges Kastner in *Le Dernier Roi de Juda* and then by Delibes, Thomas, Saint-Saëns, Bizet, and Debussy, and although Halévy incorporated a saxophone quartet in his *Le Juif errant* in 1852 (to be followed by quartets in works by Massenet, d'Indy, and Richard Strauss), the instrument met much opposition until the advent of the twentieth-century masters Marcel Mule and Sigurd Rascher, who inspired men like Glazunov, Francaix, Ibert, Martin, Pierné, and Rivier to write solo works or quartets for it. Although the interest in jazz actually had little to do with the sudden interest in the saxophone at the turn of the century, to mention the saxophone and not mention the fact of jazz virtuosi like Sidney Bechet, Coleman Hawkins, Lester Young, Charlie Parker, John Coltrane, Sonny Rollins, and Ornette Coleman would be irresponsible. Yet limitations of space forbid the mention of jazz pianists, trumpeters, and so forth: how then does one responsibly approach some of the "new music" of the new virtuosi of "Western Classical Music" when it in many ways merges with the jazz of the recent past? What about bassist Charles Mingus, Eric Dolphy and his several woodwinds? Can one talk about violinist Leroy Jenkins, and not about Stuff Smith?

As a result of the casualties of war, the piano, older and more orthodox than the saxophone, suddenly acquired a small repertory of specialized virtuoso pieces. After the pianist Paul Wittgenstein lost the use of his right arm in World War I, he commissioned works for left hand alone from Ravel, Britten, Strauss, Prokofiev, and others. Otakar Hollmann, similarly maimed in that war, commissioned Janáček's Capriccio and Martinů's Concertino (Divertissement).

In the first half of the century, some lesser-known performers collaborated with the most important composers, thereby becoming associated with some of the most significant solo compositions. For example, Samuel Dushkin, who studied with Leopold Auer and Fritz Kreisler, helped Stravinsky with technical problems in the composition of the Violin Concerto and consequently gave its first performance; subsequently, he gave the première of Stravinsky's *Duo Concertant*. Louis Krasner, a student of Carl Flesch, commissioned the Violin Concerto of Alban Berg and then gave the world première of Schoenberg's Violin Concerto.

Some of today's virtuosi have had little interest in the music of their contemporaries save those who attempt nothing more difficult than to be mildly amusing, but it would be unfair to judge these performers harshly. Some of them inspire concert attendance simply because they perform so well. So it is with Itzhak Perlman, Pinchas Zukerman, and Luciano Pavarotti, for example. Jean-Pierre Rampal and James Galway, who will play only the most accessible modern works and are unusually cavalier in their approach to older and more serious works, nevertheless are better all-round flutists than is Severino Gazzelloni, the first virtuoso of the modern flute, and they have expanded its popularity as had never been done before, despite Gazzelloni's tv superstar status in Europe.

Every now and then a virtuoso whom one thinks of as conservative will take a stab at a demanding contemporary piece. One would expect Isaac Stern, for example, to perform the Bartók Concerto, a modern classic; but what a pleasant surprise to hear him tackle a work by Krzysztof Penderecki! Gidon Kremer has championed the work of his friend Alfred Schnittke, as Glenn Gould introduced the music of his Canadian compatriots and worked hard to expose his public to the music of Schoenberg. Numerous cello pieces were born out of the friendships of Mstislav Rostropovich with Prokofiev, Shostakovich, Britten, and others. Though less well known here, Siegfried Palm has actively supported the music of his contemporaries. Maurizio Pollini often gives two recitals in close succession, one with more or less traditional programming, the other thornier, with at least one major twentieth-century or contemporary work on it.

For the first fifty years of the century then, composers might have designed works for a specific virtuoso much as Mozart had tailored arias for specific singers. Thus Edgard Varèse wrote his *Density 21.5* for the platinum flute of Georges Barrère.

But in the 1950s and sixties some specialists, like the amazing pianists Yuji Takahashi and Paul Jacobs, concentrated on the music of their own century and succeeded in realizing in a musical fashion scores whose technical problems had been judged by fellow musicians as all but impossible to resolve. And composers were quick to recognize these talented new performers. Gazzelloni inspired the Sonatine of Pierre Boulez and the *Sequenza* of Luciano Berio, now modern classics.

The outstanding oboist Heinz Holliger, a master of the music of the standard repertory of earlier times and himself a composer, has expanded the possibilities of his instrument. Many works by Boulez, Olivier Messiaen, and other composers of the European vanguard of the fifties and sixties were destined for the virtuosic Instrumental Percussion Group of Strasbourg. One must likewise mention the fabulous Paul Zukofsky, an American violinist who has performed all the violin sonatas by Charles Ives and premières of works by William Schuman, Roger Sessions, Penderecki, Earle Brown, Bruno Maderna, Charles Wuorinen, Elliott Carter, and Milton Babbitt.

Just as jazz performers leapt to mind earlier, so do the virtuosi who now begin to people the contemporary music scene, especially those imaginative exponents of neglected instruments in the classical mainstream. Perhaps the most interesting is Gary Karr, one of a family of seven bass players, who has toured as a soloist and has attempted to increase the repertory for his instrument by commissioning works from Hans Werner Henze, Gunther Schuller, Alec Wilder, and others.

A new cooperative aspect developed in the 1950s in which certain performers not only specialized in the music of their own time but formed teams with a specific composer or group of composers. Pianist and composer David Tudor worked with John Cage and composers sympathetic with the aleatory avant-garde. The voice of Cathy Berberian was the instrument for which many works were conceived by her husband, Berio, among others. Bethany Beardslee, noted for her interpretations of Schoenberg, Berg, Stravinsky, Webern, and Křenek, has inspired some of the finest work of Milton Babbitt. Yvonne Loriod, first Messiaen's student, then his second wife, became his definitive interpreter.

While the improvisatorially virtuosic Gruppe Nuova Consonanza of Rome, the Improvisation Chamber Ensemble formed by Lukas Foss, and similar ensembles played music by many composers, other groups of performers were developed by composers like Steve Reich and Philip Glass to perform only the works of their founders who, as in the rock groups from which many of their ideas derive, appear as

50

composer-performers. Particularly in the case of Reich's music, the familiarity of the ensemble with the music and with each other contributes toward the virtuosically breathtaking metronomic precision that the intricate, changing patterns require in order to be effective.

Similarly exciting can be those so-called live performances of electronically generated sounds (by the Musica Elettronica Viva, for example), either in solo or ensemble formats, or that mix electronics with traditional instruments. Performers have begun to develop an amazing virtuosity in controlling the "mechanical" elements, even capitalizing on the inherent conflict between the rigid aspects of the medium and the musician's and audience's need for flexibility of expression. The technical means, sometimes of an improvisatorial nature, for effecting these expressive possibilities often require speed, dexterity, sensitivity, and clean ensemble—in a word, virtuosity.

Finally, a new type of composer-performer has emerged, whose works combine different media and who is called a performance artist. Laurie Anderson, who studied violin but whose major training was in the visual arts, plays an electronically gadgeted fiddle, writes her own lyrics and script, projects slides she has made, and struts about the stage like a rock performer. However, the elements of her performance reveal little that is masterly. A work she wrote on commission from the American Composers Orchestra was orchestrated by someone else. Many musicians, upset by this "unprofessional" approach, had forgotten that Liszt and Gershwin similarly got help, as did the fabled violin virtuoso Jarnovick. Nevertheless, although Anderson is undoubtedly a showman, she is not a violin or vocal (or even visual) virtuoso, and her compositions leave many musicians sceptical of her musical abilities. At least Laura Dean, who choreographs, dances, and composes, is a master of her dance, which is then enhanced by her music.

Though the total effect of a work by a performance artist like Anderson, Dean, or Meredith Monk (who choreographs, plays the piano, and sings her own purposely simple, childlike material) may be intellectually stimulating or emotionally moving, there are too many rough spots in the conception or performance to apply the term "virtuosic" without distorting its meaning. It is as if something always goes awry. An amateur Wagner or Stravinsky has produced an incompletely conceived and executed *Gesamtkunstwerk:* that's not virtuosity.

Franklin's glass harmonica and special pedal pianos were valid but

51

time-bound expressions of an age infatuated with mechanical things. Few of the "special effects" of Franklin's time or of the decades that followed are extant, but the stronger piano that evolved and the music written for it have endured. Today, Harry Partch's cloud chambers and bell jars have superseded Franklin's glasses; India's sitar has replaced Turkey's Janissary music in the public ear; Alvin Lucier's Long Thin Wire, stretched over a public place, set in motion by air currents created by the passing populace, and consequently producing sounds (from loudspeakers in the public space) that its vibrations have generated electronically, may be complicated in the manner of Rube Goldberg, but they lack his humor or the virtuosic élan of playing a Bach air on a single string.

Ours is an age infatuated with electronics, but a tremendous interest in exotic sources both enriches and encruds our musical language. Composers turn to Balinese and Javanese scales and instruments, African drums, computers, Hebrew cantillation, abstract phonemes, electric guitars, cybernetic violins, neon trombone slides, television-monitor conductors, voices so over-amplified as to produce pain in the ears of the audience, kazoos, synthesizers, hubcaps, Chinese gongs, Texas flowerpots, slide shows, *objets-trouvés* as instruments, exotic clothing, basic scales and rhythms, toys, radios—all in order to produce their own share of Battle Symphonies and Ecological Cantatas. Here and there, performers have begun to master some of these new instruments although the very idea of mastery is taboo among some "experimentalists" who wish to avoid becoming "technocrats."

In recent years, a renewed interest in tonal music and a retreat from the dissonance levels of most significant music written in the past fifty to seventy-five years have been labeled, often with gross imprecision, the New Romanticism. Exemplifying that tag, *All in the Golden Afternoon,* part of David Del Tredici's series of works inspired by Lewis Carroll's *Alice,* features a virtuosic, respiteless soprano part—necessarily amplified so that it may sound without strain over the massive orchestra—that recalls the delicious pyrotechnical extravagances of Richard Strauss.

Those works that eventually may stand out from the multitude of works produced today will do so because of inherent worth (the clarity and profundity of thought as ineluctably expressed by the sole craft necessary and sufficient to express it, yet often not immediately perceivable) and because of the direction music history takes, as well

52

as the direction in which those works may push music history. The abilities of performers will help in no small way to expedite recognition of and to propagandize valuable work.

In the meantime we may have to suffer the less than lucid composers who will be known not for their music but for their tight-wire acts, which need no net because no virtuosi walk the wires and no ideas falling from them are worth catching.

—P. E.S.

Florentine woodcut, 1500; Österreichische Nationalbibliothek, Wien

Performance Practice and Interpretation

The performance of most Western music depends to a large extent on written symbols. The term, "performance practice," refers to the way in which these symbols are interpreted. But musical notation is only a shorthand whose symbols, in one situation, may simply remind performers of the details of something already known; in another, may serve as a skeleton which performers must flesh out; or, in the majority of instances, may be rather detailed instructions that indicate more or less explicitly how a composer wants his music to sound. A single musical symbol can mean different things in different eras or countries; several different symbols may all refer to the same thing; and certain symbols may refer to things restricted to a specific time and place. Because notation has evolved over hundreds of years with an apparent continuity of tradition, a performer must beware mistaking symbolic for referent identity.

The conventions of the era, nation, genre, and composer determine what aspects of sound are to be controlled and to what degree. The concern, or lack of it, with which a performer strives to understand the conventions of a work so as to interpret it within its stylistic bounds likewise depends upon the conventions of the performer's era, nation, training, and temperament.

Beyond how the score apparently limits the performer, acoustical factors like the size of the hall, its resonance, reverberation, temperature, and humidity, and the size and kind of ensemble will from performance to performance influence conscious and unconscious choices with respect to deviations in tempo, phrasing, articulation, dynamics, vibrato, timbre, and duration.

Although ambiguity and flexibility in Western music contribute to the feeling of newness on rehearing a work, they also give the performer latitude to distort the composer's intention. Aesthetic tension in most Western music arises from the conflict between the composer's intention (as expressed by his notation and to be understood within the framework of the peculiarities of person, time, and place) and the performer's interpretation (what he believes to be the composer's intention) as he brings the concrete reality of sound to the abstract designs on paper. Some performers, however, honor no obligation to the composer, only an obligation to re-create: for them the score is merely the means by which they express themselves.

Mozart expected the performer to take only those liberties granted him by the composer and to "re-create" the work in such good taste that the performer would give the impression of having composed it. But what liberties constituted good taste? Beethoven expected performers "to inject" their own feelings into a piece. But how? Time and again, musicians and composers have bemoaned the havoc virtuosi have wrought in the name of Feeling or Art.

In 1613 the tenor and theorist Domenico Cerone complained that the addition of roulades to cadences in the church music of Palestrina resembled the sound of a flock of geese. A quick glance at some comments from the English Baroque reveals great discontent: "Contrivances, which have been the result of Time and Thought, are not very likely to be improved by any performance *extempore*" (Charles Avison, 1756). Those who had not the taste or knowledge were asked to "play plain" (Matthew Locke, 1656), so as not to arouse "the disgust which this gives to some, and the surprise which it excites in all the audience" (Dr. Gregory, 1766) by "utterly destroy[ing] whatever Passion the Composer may have designed to express" (Charles Avison, 1752). In 1851, Rossini wrote succinctly of a complaint he had voiced as early as 1817: "The performers should be nothing but accurate *executants* of what is written down. . . . The composer and the poet are the only true *creators*."

As the nineteenth century progressed, composers calculated and notated more aspects of the sounds they had in mind and demanded from the performer more fidelity to the written note. Bach had been criticized for writing down too much, because Baroque performers, like jazz performers, were expected to improvise. Handel sometimes asked performers to improvise an entire movement, as in the Organ Concerto op. 7, no. 4. Beethoven loaded his scores with instructions

56

of which Bach probably had never dreamed. Berlioz, compared to Beethoven, was fanatically fussy about his instructions but in turn appears alarmingly insouciant if not outright negligent compared to Mahler, Schoenberg, Webern, and ensuing composers up to the present time. But about 1945, an opposition group headed by John Cage began a turnabout and offered the performer radically new opportunities for improvisation.

Many present-day performers only fairly recently realized that the tradition in which they were raised drastically differed from that of the Baroque period. Even though a distinct break took place between the Baroque and Classical eras, it took many years to convince these performers that Baroque conventions differed from those they had been taught and that the notes, which looked like the notes of our time, sometimes meant very different things indeed. Eventually, special performance groups devoted themselves to the problems. That battle, though not yet over, appears to be going fairly well.

It is far more difficult to persuade musicians on another front—the difference in performance practice between about 1830 and about 1910—because no clean break in tradition occurred between 1750 and 1910. The very continuity of forms, genres, instruments, melodic and rhythmic patterns, and basic harmonic language seems rather effectively to deny distinct Classical and Romantic periods and to argue for a tradition of common performance practice. Joseph Szigeti, to choose a twentieth-century violinist at random, has a tutorial genealogy that traces back through Jenö Hubay, Joseph Joachim, Joseph Böhm, and Jacques-Pierre-Joseph Rode to Jean-Baptiste Viotti, and then back further via Gaetano Pugnani and Giovanni Battista Somis to Corelli. These style-historic and pedagogical continua, valid in their own right, do not constitute necessary and sufficient proofs of a continuum of performance practice. The idea of "continuity" misleads; it is not synonymous with "identity."

Twentieth-century technology demonstrates the difference dramatically. It has permitted us to hear the teachers and teachers' teachers of today's pianists. How shocked we were in the early 1960s to hear the recordings of the Welte piano rolls made between 1905 and 1913 by Hofmann, Debussy, Ravel, Paderewski, Samaroff, Saint-Saëns, de Pachmann, Busoni, Granados, Falla, Carreño, Ganz, d'Albert, and Richard Strauss! What a revelation of late nineteenth- and early twentieth-century performance styles, after growing up with the sounds of performers only one or two generations removed! And how we had to reevaluate our idea of how tradition can veer from what we believe to be its course.

Today, we seem to know more about Baroque practice than we do about times much closer to us. Because no break in the "tradition" is evident, the prejudices are difficult to destroy. Not only the notes, the forms, the harmonies, but even the instruments are part of our training. Or are they?

Of all the instruments of our modern orchestra whose identically named kin performed Beethoven's Ninth Symphony in 1824, perhaps only the trombone is really the same. Louder, more reliable, more brilliant, and better tuned, modern flutes and oboes are also more agile owing to their Boehm key mechanisms, but they are less resonant, pastoral, calm, and sweet than the instruments for which Beethoven wrote. Likewise, his woody-sounding clarinet chuckled more than its counterpart does today.

Reliability and ease in virtuoso passages again are the criteria for the modern wide-bore rotary-valved (therefore chromatic) French horn; more German than French now, the horn has a totally different sound from its cheerful, romantic, hand-stopped narrow-bore predecessor, the true French horn (the *cor de chasse,* i.e., hunting horn, or *Waldhorn*) for which Brahms wrote his marvelous trio. The trumpets, too, had no valves. The timpani were smaller, and the triangles may have had jingling rings attached to them.

The violins and violas had no chin rests nor the cellos spikes, both of which appurtenances permit endless use of a wider, quicker vibrato. Vibrato was rare with most instruments but not forbidden for purposes of highlighting an individual note. (The Joachim Quartet may have been the first to use vibrato regularly and not solely as a special effect. Leopold Auer suggested that it be reserved for important notes.) Beethoven's viola was smaller than ours; his bow predated Tourte; his strings were made of gut, not metal; and his bowing and phrasing signs require different readings from ours, just as do his dots, wedges, trills, and graces.

The pitch level then was from one-half to a whole step lower than it is today, which means, among other things, that vocalists had less of a struggle with their parts. Even Beethoven's metronome markings cannot be trusted: we believe he probably forgot to wind the spring. Beethoven's performance of his Ninth would undoubtedly sound very different from Bernstein's.

The piano itself had not yet matured as an instrument, and perfor-

58

mance on it initially followed general keyboard practice. Johann Nepomuk Hummel, a fine composer and one of the great virtuoso pianists of his time, had studied under Mozart; in 1827 he wrote that Mozart did not use the pedal when he played. We know from Mozart's own writing that he expected a pianist to use correct fingering and to have a smooth, flexible execution and a quiet, steady hand, so as to produce a melodic line that "flowed like oil."

Beethoven loved several Mozart concerti. How might he have played them? Carl Czerny, a pupil of Beethoven, insisted on strict time, but Anton Schindler, Beethoven's biographer and friend, described Beethoven's playing as romantically free. Antoine Reicha, a friend of Beethoven, wrote of a concert that took place in Vienna, probably some time between 1803 and 1809. What would Mozart have thought of Beethoven's performance? Reicha's account reflects either upon Beethoven's interpretation or upon the pianos of his day. "At court, Beethoven performed a Mozart piano concerto and asked me to turn the pages for him. At every moment the piano strings broke, leaping into the air, and the hammers got stuck among them. But Beethoven, wanting at all cost to finish the piece, asked me to disengage the hammers one by one as they came to a standstill and to clear away the broken strings. To [accomplish] all that, I had more to do than Beethoven, because I had to jump up constantly and beat about the piano for the whole piece."

Liszt shattered pianos everywhere, often keeping one in reserve at his concerts. Nineteenth-century musicians were not the first to ravage instruments: Pietro Locatelli (1695–1764), whose work may have influenced Paganini, did wonders with double stops and *scordatura*, thereby achieving the "impossible," but he played with such ferocity that he reputedly went through dozens of violins each year.

Mozart had expected melodic lines to "flow like oil," but much, then as now, flowed like snake oil. Leopold Mozart had advertised in 1763 that Wolfgang would perform on a harpsichord whose keyboard was completely covered by a thin cloth so that he could not see the keys, as if an accomplished keyboardist didn't play by feel.

A cloth-covered keyboard was a cheap way to attract an audience. But after all, musicians hark back to jugglers. On 23 December 1806 the internationally renowned violinist Franz Clement gave the première of Beethoven's Violin Concerto at a gala concert in Vienna's Theater-an-der-Wien, of which Clement was director. An overture by Méhul preceded the concerto. The first part of the concert also

Engraving, 1777, J.R. Holzhalb; Zentralbibliothek, Zürich

included an air by Mozart and was completed by fragments from Handel's *Ode for Saint Cecilia's Day,* orchestrated by Mozart. The second half contained an overture, a vocal quartet by Cherubini, another fragment from Handel's *Ode,* and a fantasia by Clement.

One report has it that Clement played the concerto at sight without previous rehearsal. One reason may be that Beethoven supposedly never finished commissioned works until the last minute. (He followed in good footsteps: on 12 May 1789 Mozart performed two unrehearsed concerti in Leipzig. He reassured the orchestra that "the parts are written out correctly; you play right and so do I.") Other performers held only orchestral rehearsals because they were loath to reveal their own tricks.

Descriptions disagree somewhat on whether Beethoven's concerto was performed in toto on the first half or divided between the two halves, and whether the fantasia was played after Beethoven's first movement, between the second and third movement, or at the end of the concert, each possibility an accepted practice of the time. In his fantasia Clement improvised on his violin and then played a sonata of his own, bowing a single string while holding his violin upside down. Against such odds, it is no wonder that Beethoven's three-movement work for four strings (to be played upright) had few subsequent performances until Joachim took up its cause.

German-speaking countries in particular distinguished between the serious, art-promoting local music societies and the rare concerts of touring musicians whose playing may have been exceptionally brilliant but also superficial. The Prague nobility looked down on the pianist Daniel Steibelt, for example, who, they deemed, lacked imagination in playing, despite his bravura; they did not care for his fanciful titles and programmatic ideas. But he won over their women with the woman he claimed was his wife; she accompanied him on the tambourine in some pieces. In the following days she would give a twelve-lesson course at twelve gold ducats (the concert ticket itself had cost one ducat), and she received an additional twelve ducats for each tambourine she sold. Steibelt remained in Prague several weeks, and the couple sold a wagonload of instruments.

Concerts were shambles. People met there, talked, and greeted one another across the room. The concert manager would bang the side of the harpsichord to quiet them; that put the instrument out of tune. A pseudonymously signed article, appearing in a paper of 18 August 1802, argued that because the artist cannot do without the masses, free art had been made servile; the taste for music spreads rapidly but taste in it declines, the writer concluded.

Descriptive pieces had a long history, and especially noisy ones arrived during and after the French Revolution and Napoleonic wars. But the work for which the word "warhorse" might well have been coined saw the light of day before then: "The Battle of Prague," published in London in 1790, was for piano (and other instruments if available). It imitated the sounds of war, its performer being called upon to give "the word of command." A certain Miss Hoffman, after performing at Windsor Castle, seems to have flung down the gauntlet in 1792 accompanied on kettledrums by her brother; she was six, he three and a half. "The Battle of Prague" infested continental programs for decades but was popular among Anglophones world-wide for over half a century. The work's composer, Franz Kotzwara (really Kočvara), came to London from Bohemia via the continent ca. 1788 and achieved fame solely by virtue of the "Battle" and the bizarre manner of his death: accidental hanging in a London bordello while probably attempting autoerotic asphyxiation.

In the 1830s "The Battle of Prague" appeared on the programs of one of the most famous pianists in Europe, Marie Pleyel, the Mlle. Moke with whom Berlioz had been hopelessly in love but who instead married the more "solid" Camille Pleyel, son of Ignaz, the then famous composer, fine pianist, publisher, and piano manufacturer. A student of Henri Herz, Moscheles, and Kalkbrenner—all pianistic lions—Marie Moke, while involved with Berlioz in 1830, wisely claimed to love the music of Beethoven, but her programs were filled with Rossini's *Regata,* the "Rataplan" and "The Blessing of the Daggers" from Meyerbeer's *Huguenots,* "A Naval Battle," and "The Battle of Nerwinde"—with trumpet calls, cannonades (produced by indistinctly hitting the bass notes with flattened hands), cries of the wounded and dying, and victorious fanfares. Extra pedals on the piano controlled a set of drums, triangle, and cymbals.

This was not an aberration solely of the French or the Romantics; eighteenth-century German pianos had several such devices because musicians, interested in color, amusement, and oddities, searched for new or curious ways to produce them. Curt Sachs writes of some Viennese pianos with as many as six pedals including a bassoon pedal, which pressed a strip of wood lined with tissue paper against the bass strings so that they rattled, and a Turkish music pedal which operated a triangle, cymbals, and a drumstick hitting the sound board. This latter pedal imitated Janissary music, which had cap-tured the imagination of eighteenth-century Europe as the sitar has captivated so many in our century. (Beethoven accompanies the tenor solo in the finale of his Ninth Symphony with Janissary music.) More recently, Charles Ives called for a "drum-corps" effect in the piano, in the manner of "The Battle of Nerwinde," at the end of the second movement of his Second Violin Sonata. In the first decade of the twentieth century, Henry Cowell sought new sounds inside the piano, experiments picked up and expanded upon later by John Cage and other twentieth-century composers.

Only in the 1830s did the piano itself begin to approach the modern instrument in strength and tone. After years of experiments—with shapes, pedals, pin blocks, bridges, action, string tension, hammers, and wire strings—an American invention of 1825, the complete cast-iron frame, and subsequent improvements upon it for the next fifty years, gave the piano its modern strength and flexibility. Just as Chopin shunned the large concert hall in favor of the intimate salon, so he avoided the concert-grand out of preference for its medium-sized relative.

But not only had the instrument changed; so did the method of performing on it. Chopin's fingering stems from the clavichord style described by C.P.E. Bach in his "Essay on the True Art of Playing Keyboard Instruments" (1753), a style passed on in Bach's students J.C. Bach and J.L. Dussek through Mozart, Haydn, Beethoven, Clementi, Hummel, J.B. Cramer, and John Field. Carl Czerny, however, who did not approve of the eighteenth century theory of touch which recognized differing strengths and capabilities of the fingers, taught that all fingers should be treated equally; by so doing he effected a stylistic revolution, paving the way for Liszt.

The virtuoso-conductor did not become a regular part of the orchestral scene until at least mid-century. Although examples of a violinist or keyboardist occasionally waving a roll of paper appear in the late eighteenth century, the idea did not catch on until the 1830s and forties and then met with resistance in some quarters. Until then, "conducting" meant directing preparations for the concert and playing the score at the piano (which had replaced the harpsichord) while facing the orchestra in the pit, and alternately waving one's arms or clapping.

Simultaneously, the violinist at the first desk (i.e., the concertmaster, or leader) "led" (without benefit of score) by playing from his part, letting his movements give the beat, or tapping his bow against the stand or stamping his foot when his movements failed to produce the proper result. The bassist Dragonetti was known for helping out by accenting the bass line, and this no doubt suggests that other double-bass players or strong personalities in other parts of the small orchestras of the time did similar duty.

Engraving, ca. 1785; Musées de la Ville de Strasbourg

In the opera or when choral voices were added to the orchestral components, a time-beater was used; he sometimes tapped the floor audibly with a large staff. With two, three, or four sources for audible or visual beat, clean ensemble and attacks must have been rare indeed. (In Paris, the leader had always held sway except at Opéra, where a contest might ensue between leader and time-beater, who still reigned despite the grotesque example set by Lully in 1867. He banged his toe with the staff, infection set in, and gangrene brought about the composer's final cadence.) By the 1860s, complaints already circulated about conductors who were not simply beating time but who were interpreting.

The orchestral piano, as successor to the harpsichord, did not retain the harpsichord's role as continuo instrument. The piano's sound, though it did not mix well with that of the orchestra, had nevertheless been added to it by the "conductor," and eventually the instrument became no more than a desk for him whose own function was being taken up more and more by the leader. The other vestige from the continuo, the bass melody instrument, had its role somewhat reinterpreted by the Yorkshire cello virtuoso, Robert Lindley, partner to Dragonetti at London's Royal Opera House; Lindley elegantly and fancifully accompanied the recitatives with brilliant arpeggios and delicate sustained tones.

The discipline of musicology, born as a result of the nineteenth century's interest in the past, fostered the idea of the *Urtext,* the so-called original version. The concept of authenticity was very much on the minds of nineteenth-century musicians, although, like much else in that century, its contradiction was close at hand. Editorial attitudes reflect virtuosic attitudes because editor and virtuoso often were one. The supposed worship of the original text does not seem consistent with editorial practice because the editors made changes without indicating what they had done or that they had done so. In other instances, the reasons given for changes are identical with those heard today from self-proclaimed highly sensitive performers whose stylistic sensitivities are distinctly ahistoric.

As an editor, Liszt wanted to give the performer greater license and to increase effects without changing the composer's style [!] The works he edited he appropriately [!] rewrote for modern piano—the composer would be pleased with it, goes his argument—to avoid quibbling and pretentiousness and to make a practical edition by adding fingering and pedal marks. In short, the editorial practices, their results still polluting the shelves of the marketplace and the boards of the concert hall, were abominable: octaves added, measures inserted, notes altered to solve technical problems or to "correct" apparent errors, and notational changes to make rhythmic structures "clearer," all in the name of a "practical edition."

The distinguished pianist Adolph von Henselt edited a Weber sonata and added melody, harmony, "richness," octaves, and virtuoso difficulties to those in the original. Whereas Henselt elaborated upon Weber, the German cellist Friedrich Wilhelm Ludwig Grützmacher assembled a pasticcio of pieces by Luigi Boccherini, himself a virtuoso cellist. The confection has come down to us ironically as

65

Boccherini's best known cello concerto, the one in B-flat. Renowned in his own time, Grützmacher, like many other virtuosi who were not able composers but who sought public acclaim through cheap tricks, has faded from general knowledge, even in musically literate circles; but he remains notorious in the footnotes of the works of specialists, in part because of his outrageous "concert adaptations" of Boccherini.

Because many great composers were extemporizers as well as agile performers, their fame rested in part on their unwritten work. Fortunately, C.P.E. Bach, the greatest improvisor of his day, wrote works, as did several earlier Baroque composers, with written-out embellished repeats, free fantasies, and improvised variations, works that he intended for his students as models of the art. But fewer opportunities arise for elaborate embellishment and extended improvisation in the written music of the late eighteenth and nineteenth centuries.

Far from leaving us models of his art, Mozart improvised so much of his music that his piano concertos, written for himself, contain some pages whose passages cry out for further embellishment. Hummel, his student, brought out an edition of Mozart's concerti with heavy embellishment. One assumes that Hummel knew the style and had the taste to do it properly, but he unfortunately lacked his teacher's imagination. Even if in no other way, Mozart concerti present formidable challenges to taste. Beethoven's scores probably are more complete.

But Paganini's scores again tell us next to nothing. He really was not a "composer"; he was a top-flight sight-reader, a fine musician, a master of his instrument who never revealed his secrets, and probably the world's greatest improvisor. He performed other composers' ideas literally in their tutti sections, he said, but in solo passages he gave free reign "in the Italian manner" to his imagination. Add virtuosic performance practice (in this case improvisation) to editorial practice and imagine what might result—talk about painting the lily!

Reverence for the text? No, once again. The text was a challenge to the performer's ingenuity and creativity. The black virtuoso violinist George Bridgetower gave the première of Beethoven's "Kreutzer" Sonata in 1803. The work's original dedicatee (but dropped because of a battle "over a girl"), Bridgetower left a note in the manuscript, "When I accompanied him in the Sonata-Concertante. . .", and then showed how he improvised an embellishment that Beethoven approved.

66

Drawing, 1834, Moritz von Swind; Universitatsbibliothek, Kiel

The title page of the original manuscript is informative. It reads (in translation): "Sonata for the pianoforte and a violin obbligato written in a brilliant, very *concertante* style, almost like a concerto." In the chamber music of the late eighteenth century, sonatas for keyboard and other instruments were actually for keyboard with the accompaniment of the other instruments. The "Kreutzer" Sonata apparently is a transition piece; still, the violin "accompanies" the keyboard, but it is obbligato, in fact, almost like a concerto. (Incidentally, Beethoven dropped the word *brillant,* which obstinately recurs in the works of other composers in the nineteenth century.)

The finale of Chopin's op. 58 exists in Liszt's hand and shows many changes made either for himself or for his students. Both Liszt and Chopin apparently varied their own music from performance to performance, yet Chopin complained that Liszt rarely performed exactly what was written. Liszt has been reported to have added trills and tremolos to the first movement of Beethoven's *Moonlight* Sonata in Paris in 1832. As late as the 1870s, Ferdinand David, student of Spohr, close friend of Mendelssohn, and teacher of Joachim and August Wilhelm, introduced varied repeats in his performances of chamber music by Mozart and Haydn. Dussek had specified that no ornaments were to be added to one of his most important sonatas, a prescription whose presence proves the general practice.

When the educated and esteemed Ignaz Moscheles heard an elaborate performance of one of his own pieces by Liszt, he admitted that it was more Liszt than Moscheles but would not have had it any other way. (It has been said that the English are not incompetent cooks; they really like their food that way.) Nineteenth-century musicians had to tamper with texture, free the rhythm, and intensify the expression; no one escaped unscathed, not Bach, Mozart, Grieg, Mendelssohn, nor Schumann.

For performers who hadn't the genius of Mozart, the only place for significant improvisation had lain in the cadenza of the concerto, but after Beethoven's Fifth Piano Concerto, this held true only in some display concerti and a few other isolated cases.

The word "cadenza" comes from "cadence," which means the final series of notes with which a phrase, section, or entire work arrives at its logical conclusion. The practice of inserting a roulade, flourish, or brief coloratura passage—a cadenza—before, in, or after the cadence goes back at least as far as eighth- or ninth-century plainchant in which the long melismatic vocalization, called the *jubilus,* accompanies the final vowel of "alleluia." Similar treatment occurs in stock melodies of the ancient Greeks and in divers folk musics. The cadenza as we generally conceive it seems to belong to Baroque opera and to the instrumental music of Corelli and the composers of the ensuing century.

When Moscheles, Sigismond Thalberg, and Mendelssohn played Bach's Concerto in D minor for Three Keyboards (BWV 1063) on three pianos in London in 1844, each performer improvised a long cadenza. In this nineteenth-century version of the "duels" of Baroque organists, Mendelssohn's cadenza was judged most apt, Thalberg's the poorest.

The cadenza became a composed showpiece with little if any artistic value. The virtuosi or teachers who wrote the "standard" cadenzas for Mozart and Beethoven concerti knew their instruments but not how to compose music.

Mozart's written cadenzas may not have been meant to be inserted

68

into his concerti for his own use but were models of the kind of thing he did or wanted his students to do; they were simple, not Terminal Development sections, and, like Beethoven's own cadenzas, they were not obligatory. Beethoven composed cadenzas for the first and third movements of one of his favorite Mozart concerti, the D-minor (K.466), perhaps for the use of his student Ferdinand Ries— Beethoven himself would have improvised on the spot.

Abraham Veinus notes that the modern cadenza is "that part of the concerto where the orchestra stops playing and the listener . . . stops listening, so that all . . . may concentrate upon the bag of tricks which the performer as wizard-virtuoso (not as maker of music) is to trot out for inspection." In 1766 a certain Dr. Gregory similarly observed that "the long flourish at the close of a song, and sometimes at other periods of it," serves the performer to "shew the utmost compass of his throat and execution, and all that is required, is, that he should conclude in the proper key; the performer . . . shew[s] the audience the extent of his abilities, by the most fantastical and unmeaning extravagance of execution."

Since Beethoven, some composers have written cadenzas and made them part and parcel of the concerto; others have done away with them entirely. Mendelssohn, who had left cadenzas out of his piano concerti, wrote one for the violin concerto with the help of Ferdinand David, who premiered it. Mendelssohn's cadenza maintains continuity of thought by functioning as a transition from the Development to the Recapitulation rather than as an embellishment of the final cadence. Schumann's piano concerto maintains a freedom similar to Mendelssohn's and somewhat follows its plan, but, like Berlioz's work for orchestra and solo viola obbligato, *Harold in Italy,* Schumann's deliberately proceeds anti-virtuosically: its cadenza (Schumann's own), though occurring at the traditional place, nevertheless sustains the mood.

The overwrought concern for self-expression in the nineteenth century led composers to search out new and more subtle or dramatic effects, which had to be made explicit in their notation; the same concern permitted performers to disregard that notation. The ensuing developments in the twentieth century followed no linear pattern: contradictory aesthetic movements co-existed for years, almost unaware of each other, or the warring antithetical movements merged and created new antitheses as if they were Hegelian guerrillas. Composers regularly challenged the techniques of the performer and

Woodcut, 1889; Illustrirte Zeitung, *Leipzig*

demanded greater fidelity to their ideas. In the first several decades of the twentieth century, composers like Poulenc, Stravinsky, and Hindemith even asked that their music be played without any expression at all; the former two dispensed, in a sense, with the performer by writing for player piano. Varèse, about 1922, hoped that a time would come when composer and electrician together could replace the performers, who, through inability or disinclination to follow directions, got in the way of the communication between composer and listener. The tape recorder, computers, and synthesizers appear to have realized that dream.

As the new century continued, faithfulness to the score became increasingly important. Of course stylistic differences existed. Horowitz, whose very name is synonymous with virtuosity, is noted for his steely brilliance and clarity. A specialist in Liszt, Tchaikovsky, Rachmaninoff, and Scriabin, he gravitated toward the more lyrical, romantic, and conservative composers of his own century, Poulenc, Prokoviev, and Barber. Yet like a nineteenth-century pianist Horowitz brought the house down with his encores (vestiges of nineteenth-century practice), his paraphrase of *Carmen,* and his transcription of "Stars and Stripes Forever." A warmer temperament was evident in the bravura performances of Arthur Rubinstein, who made specialties of Chopin and Spanish music. How different was Walter Gieseking, who exemplified his bi-national background by performing in both German and French repertory with equal understanding. His tone scintillated, but unlike Horowitz and Rubinstein he was never flashy. Of still different natures are the "scholarly" pianists, Serkin and Schnabel, for whom the composer always came first.

After 1950 the widespread distribution of high-fidelity long-playing records (so faithful to instrumental sounds that one heard noises usually inaudible in the concert hall) permitted easier comparison of performers, although studio performance cannot be compared with recital hall performance. "Close recording" made it possible to bring the intimate early music groups into the living room along with musicological research and attitudes (incorporated in the liner notes) which previously had been hidden in scholarly journals.

A more knowledgeable audience, its historical appetites newly whetted, required less flamboyant performances and more respect for the text. What would the pseudonymous writer of 1802 have had to say about that development?

At about the same time (post-World War II) that some composers sought total control over every aspect of musical expression, others were beginning to give performers more room for "interpretation" than they had ever had: chance music had arrived, and brand new instrumental and vocal performing techniques were evolving, including a more theatrical approach that often involved the audience. Notation therefore blossomed to the point where many pieces had their own notational systems, designed to deal with the idiosyncratic problems of a particular work and with methods of inducing chance in one area while limiting it in another—for example, notating specific rhythms and dynamics but only a melodic profile for which any notes may be used within a given range of a specific instrument. The resultant scores were influenced not a little by the graphic artistry and ingenuity of the composer.

Thus, a certain degree of performance specialization set in. Some performers are apt at bringing off with breathtaking ease stringent notated demands of composers. Others can improvise with alacrity in the idioms of the composers of their choice. Still others perform in conjunction with electronic means. Some composers call for a combination of these talents.

As far as the music of the past is concerned, "authenticity" in performance can never be complete. The aesthetic theories of some music (medieval, for example) do not conform to our idea of authenticity because only the idea matters, not its realization. In the search for authenticity, some questions will probably remain unanswered and some answers may be impractical to achieve. To assemble an orchestra for a Beethoven symphony that would use original instruments or modern copies and to train the performers to use them properly is an expensive proposition.

It would be a cruel fiat indeed that banned Bach from the pianist's repertory. But the Fifth Brandenburg cries out for the harpsichord; the piano, while it can sound all the notes, does not balance with the other instruments, nor is it crisp or thrilling enough. Some musicians would tell us that our ears, our tastes, and our expectations are different from those of other times. Do we *want* to hear late nineteenth-century music played in the manner of the late nineteenth century, where singers slide from note to note and pianists anticipate the beats of a slow movement with their left hand? These objections or questions sound suspiciously like those made with regard to performance of Baroque and Renaissance music before modern performers mastered the instruments and their idioms.

What a composer writes down is in effect only what he believes cannot be taken for granted in the sonorous, harmonic, rhythmic, melodic, and formal practices of his time. For the work to be re-created, its performance practice must be understood. To perform a work by Schumann without knowing what he expected his notations to produce will result in music that may or may not be pleasant or moving or successful, but it will not be the work that Schumann wrote.

—P. E. S.

72

Notes on the Selections

Pablo Casals

SIDE 1 BAND 1

Johann Sebastian Bach (1685–1750)
Cello Suite no. 3 in C major, BWV 1009
      I. Praeludium
     II. Allemande
   III. Courante
   IV. Sarabande
    V. Bourrée I & II
   VI. Gigue

Casals, cello.
Recorded November 1936, London. Included through the courtesy of EMI Records, Ltd.

This collection could have no more appropriate beginning than
Casals playing Bach. The great Catalan musician Pablo (born Pau)
Casals lived to the age of ninety-six (1876–1973) and was active as
both composer and performer for more than eight full decades.
Through all those years the Bach suites for unaccompanied cello,
which had been ignored if not totally unknown until he became their
champion, constituted a sort of core, an artistic and spiritual testament, for Casals as man and musician.

    Casals was not the first famous cellist, but he is credited with hav-
ing refined and elevated the art of playing the cello in such a way as
to realize for the first time the instrument's inherent nobility in terms
of sheer tonal beauty as well as expressive qualities. (It might be

remembered that in 1740, two years before Boccherini's birth, a French writer denounced the cello as "a miserable beggar, a tatterdemalion and a poor devil," and that 150 years later, before Casals was heard in Britain, Bernard Shaw compared the instrument unfavorably with "a bee buzzing in a stone jug.") Casals began experimenting with new fingering and bowing techniques when he was only eleven years old and made his formal debut three years later in Barcelona. He had discovered the Bach suites more or less by accident the previous year; his response to this music was to remain perhaps the strongest single factor in determining the path he would follow.

Casals had a colorful career as a teen-ager, attracting influential patrons and also performing in cafes and music halls in Paris and Barcelona. Before he was twenty he began teaching in Barcelona, he was first cellist in that city's principal orchestra, and he formed a trio with the pianist-composer Enrique Granados and the Belgian violinist Mathieu Crickboom. In 1905 he founded a more celebrated and longer-lived trio with two French colleagues, pianist Alfred Cortot and violinist Jacques Thibaud. Fourteen years later Casals confirmed his seriousness as a conductor by creating his own orchestra in Barcelona.

Because of his firm stand toward the Franco regime in his native country and his outspokenness on the human condition in general, Casals came to be regarded as a great moral force as well as a great musician, representing to many—both within and outside the world of music—humanity's conscience. His festivals at Prades and Perpignan in the early 1950s, and subsequently in Puerto Rico, were convocations of musicians who shared his own exceptional level of commitment to both artistic and humanitarian ideals. In his nineties he still performed and recorded at the Marlboro Festival in Vermont.

Through those many decades of productive activity and the years of "renunciation" of an active career because of his uncompromising political idealism, the Bach suites remained a unique source of strength for Casals, as well as a unique challenge. He began every day of his life by playing one of the six suites for himself. His procedure would be to work through the entire set of six suites (not necessarily in numerical order) from Monday through Saturday, and then on Sunday to go over the one suite that had given him the most problems. He resisted requests to prepare his own performing edition of the cello suites, because his own approach to them was constantly deepening and expanding and he felt there could be no "definitive"

Pablo Casals   NYPL

version of such works. Fortunately, though, he did commit them all
to records, as he did several other essential parts of the cello repertory.

Casals's activity in the recording studio, as both cellist and conductor, spanned more than a half-century, beginning in the pre-electrical
era and extending into the stereophonic. It seems especially apt that
the years 1936–39 should have been the time for his only recordings
of music as personally meaningful to him as the Bach suites. This was
an extremely dramatic time in his life, the years between his depar-
ture from Spain, where he faced a threat of execution for his opposition to the new regime, and the outbreak of World War II hastened by
the Fascist victory in his own country. (It was at the beginning of this
period, too, in 1936, that he made his matchless recording of the
Dvořák Concerto with George Szell and the Czech Philharmonic
Orchestra.) "Uncompromising," a term already used in reference to

Casals's political idealism, is no less apt in describing the integrity of his commitment to these works. In the case of another performer, one might say "He made them his own," but in speaking of Casals one can only say that he gave himself to the music, day in and day out, in an unending quest for deeper and deeper understanding.

The six suites for unaccompanied cello, numbered 1007–1012 in Wolfgang Schmieder's thematic catalogue of Bach's works, were composed about 1720, in the middle of his tenure as *Kapellmeister* to the young Prince Leopold of Anhalt-Cöthen. It was during those years (1717–23), which Bach regarded as the happiest in his life, that he produced the great bulk of his virtuoso instrumental music, including the Brandenburg Concertos and the concertos, sonatas, and partitas for violin as well as at least two of the four suites for orchestra. No one had written music of such substance for solo cello before, and there have been precious few additions to this repertory since Bach's time worthy to stand with these suites. (Indeed, the only one that comes to mind as having been generally acknowledged is the Sonata, op. 8, composed by Zoltán Kodály in 1915.) For more than a century after Bach's death, the cello suites were neglected because they were considered "academic" or pedagogical works. Even after Casals began playing them frequently in the 1890s, various musicians sought to make them more accessible by adding keyboard accompaniment—gratuitous embellishments which, fortunately, have been forgotten now. (Bach himself arranged the Fifth Suite as a lute work but preserved in that transcription his original conception of the music in terms of *solo* performance.) Each of the six suites comprises a prelude and five dance movements, the only differences among them being the appearance of a pair of bourrées as the penultimate movement in nos. 3 and 4, in place of the pair of minuets in the other four suites. In terms of sheer melodic appeal, there can be no question that the Third Suite, in C major, is the richest and most ingratiating of all.

Casals's recordings of all six Bach suites are available now in Angel set CB-3786. His Dvořák Concerto, with Szell and the Czech Philharmonic, is on Seraphim 60240, together with his 1937 recording of Bruch's *Kol Nidrei* with the London Symphony Orchestra under Sir Landon Ronald. All the recordings made by the Cortot/Thibaud/Casals trio between 1926 and 1928 are in circulation on LP now. Beethoven's *Archduke* Trio, the Haydn Trio in G major (no. 25), the Schubert in B-flat (op. 99/D. 898), and the Trios in D minor by Mendelssohn (op. 49) and Schumann (op. 63) are in Opal set 815/6, while the same performance of the *Archduke* is available with Beethoven's Variations on *"Ich bin der Schneider Kakadu"* on Seraphim 60242.

Most of Casals's postwar recordings are also available now. His own *Song of the Birds,* pieces by Couperin and Schumann, and the Mendelssohn D minor Trio, recorded at the White House in 1961 during a performance for President Kennedy, with violinist Alexander Schneider and pianist Mieczyslaw Horszowski, are on CBS AKL-5726. (The Mendelssohn is more readily obtainable, with a different coupling, on MP-38763.) All the Beethoven cello sonatas and variations, with Rudolf Serkin at the piano, are in Odyssey set 32 36 0016. The Schumann Concerto with Eugene Ormandy conducting, and Schumann's *Fünf Stücke im Volkston,* with Leopold Mannes, piano, are on Odyssey 32 16 0027, and a treasury of performances from the Prades and Perpignan festivals of 1950–52 (the Bach cello sonatas with Paul Baumgartner, piano; the Brahms Sextet, op. 18, with Isaac Stern et al.; Mozart piano concertos with Myra Hess and Rudolf Serkin; and others) has been assembled in CBS set M5X-32768. In another CBS five-disc set, under the heading *Tribute to Pablo Casals* (M5-30069), are recordings ranging from the prewar Boccherini Concerto in B-flat with Landon Ronald, Beethoven's Sonata op. 69 with Otto Schulhof, and the Brahms F major Sonata with Horszowski to the Schubert String Quintet with Stern & Co. from Perpignan and a 1969 Brahms Haydn Variations with Casals conducting the Marlboro Festival Orchestra.

A later performance of the Schubert Quintet, recorded with the Végh Quartet in stereo during the Prades Festival of 1961, is available on Turnabout TV 34407. Two live performances of Beethoven's music given at the Beethoven Haus in 1959, with Sándor Végh, violin, and Horszowski, are on Turnabout TV 34490: the Trio in C minor, op. 1, no. 3, and the cello version of the Horn Sonata, op. 17.

As conductor, Casals is represented further in stereo in a recording of his own oratorio *El pesebre* from the Festival Casals in Puerto Rico (CBS M2-32966) and in several works with the Marlboro Festival Orchestra. Among the Marlboro items, all on CBS, are Bach's four Suites for Orchestra (M2S-755) and Brandenburg Concertos (M2S-731), Beethoven's Symphony no. 7 (MY-37233), and Mozart's last six symphonies (D3S-817).

Wanda Landowska

SIDE 1 BAND 2

Johann Sebastian Bach (1685–1750)
Italian Concerto in F major, BWV 971
    I.
    II. Andante
    III. Presto

Landowska, harpsichord.
Recorded September 1936, Paris. Included through the courtesy of EMI Records, Ltd.

Although Mozart and Haydn both wrote for the harpsichord in
their early chamber music, and more or less expected it to be used in
the continuo in their early symphonies, the instrument was superseded during their time by the new one known variously as forte-
piano, Hammerflügel, and pianoforte. During the century or so in
which the piano was enlarged upon and refined to the standard proportions we know today, the harpsichord was virtually forgotten, and
in performances of eighteenth-century music it came to be either
replaced by the piano or, in continuo use, simply omitted. Even such
ensembles as the Busch Chamber Players, formed to present 'the
works of Bach and Handel, generally ignored the harpsichord; in the
Busch performances of the Brandenburg Concertos, Rudolf Serkin
played a piano. But the harpsichord did not have to wait for the Big
Baroque Boom that came after World War II for its return: well
before Serkin started performing with the Busches, Wanda Landowska, following on the less concentrated late-nineteenth-century
efforts of Arnold Dolmetsch and others, had brought the harpsichord
back—and not only for the performance of early music but as a viable
participant in the music of her own time. Manuel de Falla, Francis
Poulenc, and many other distinguished composers created new works
for Landowska, and because of her pioneering the harpsichord
became more and more a fact of contemporary musical life, playing a
part in works as diverse as the jazz-flavored octets of Alec Wilder and
the Double Concerto of Elliott Carter. It is probably not exaggerating
at all to say that without Landowska's efforts we not only would not

Wanda Landowska   NYPL

have seen the rebirth of the harpsichord as a generally accepted and, in fact, indispensable instrument, but the farther ranging interest in the "authentic instruments" of Baroque and early Classical music would have been a longer time coming.

Landowska (1879–1959) originally planned to be a pianist and, in fact, continued to perform and record on the piano to the end of her life. It was her fascination with the music of Rameau, Couperin, Scarlatti, and Bach that led her to investigate the harpsichord shortly after she arrived in Paris, already recognized as a pianist, in 1900. By 1903 she was performing a single piece on the harpsichord in each of her piano recitals. The harpsichords available for use then were crude, but she persuaded the celebrated piano-maker Pleyel to undertake the construction of an "authentic" instrument for her which she introduced to the public at a Bach festival in Breslau in 1912. Even then she had a great deal to teach herself about authentic performance style—about ornamentation, registration, tempi, and so forth—and her study continued to the last day of her life. (Actually, the harpsichords Pleyel made for Landowska had certain updated construction features and a somewhat bigger tone than what we recognize now as an authentic eighteenth-century harpsichord; most of the new works composed for her were designed for her own instrument, and several present difficulties on a truly authentic, or period, harpsichord.)

While others were encouraged by Landowska to take up the harpsichord during the 1930s, many of course had their own ideas about interpretation, and more than a few "Bach specialists" chose to stick to the modern piano. One of the better-known such specialists insisted on discussing her views with Landowska in a fairly aggressive manner, and Landowska had to bring the confrontation to an end with the acid-sweet remark: "That's all right, my dear, you continue to play Bach your way, and I'll continue to play Bach Bach's way." It always sounded like Bach's way, or Scarlatti's way, or Rameau's way, when Landowska played. It was not that she had no personality as a performer, but rather that, as all really great performing artists do, she put her own personality thoroughly and entirely at the service of the music. Although she re-recorded several of the major works in her repertory after the onset of the microgroove era, she made only one recording of Bach's Italian Concerto, on 78s in 1936. The recording is quite realistic for its time, and especially well focused: we can hear what both hands are doing at all times, and what they are doing is giving us a superbly stylish and enlivening realization of this understandably much-favored piece—and without any of the sentimentalizing that so many performers have found impossible to resist in the slow movement.

This Concerto in the Italian Style is one of several keyboard concertos by Bach that are not concertos in the generally accepted sense of a work for solo instrument with orchestra, but that are in fact thoroughly orchestral in concept, with the "orchestral accompaniment" simply incorporated into the solo part itself—forerunners, in this sense, of Liszt's piano reductions of orchestral works and of the sonata Schumann labeled Concerto without Orchestra. The violin concertos of Vivaldi are generally regarded as Bach's models in creating these works, and indeed some of them are direct transcriptions of Vivaldi concertos. The Italian Concerto, however, is a thoroughly original composition on a somewhat grander scale and in a more expansive spirit than any of the actual Italian models Bach used elsewhere. The alternation of loud and soft passages in the two outer movements reinforces the notion of alternating solo and orchestral sections, while the central slow movement is a sort of cantilena with the "accompaniment" markedly reduced, as in actual concerted works of the period. In all three movements, by no means incidentally, the themes themselves represent Bach at his highest and happiest level of melodic inventiveness.

The Italian Concerto and more elaborate Overture in the French Manner together constitute Part II of the *Clavier Übung* ("Keyboard Practice"), a series of four collections of works Bach published at the age of fifty with the intention that they would serve didactic purposes for fellow musicians but also, as he pointedly inscribed each of the four parts, "for the spiritual enjoyment of music lovers." The Italian Concerto, which has been providing that spiritual enjoyment so abundantly for the last forty years or so, did not always enjoy this sort of popularity; that it does so now is in large part because of the enthusiasm of two exceptional musicians who championed it in the 1930s: Artur Schnabel, who, like Edwin Fischer and Rudolf Serkin, brought the most penetrating insights to the performance of Bach on the modern piano, and Landowska, who revealed the unique character of such works on the instrument for which Bach himself composed them.

Landowska recorded a great deal of her harpsichord repertory and several works of Mozart and Haydn on the piano as well. Her great interpretation of the Goldberg Variations, recorded for RCA in excellent monophonic sound in 1945, has recently been reissued (AGM 1-5251), as has an outstanding Scarlatti collection (Seraphim 6139), but her equally notable performances of *The Well-Tempered Clavier,* the Two- and Three-Part Inventions, and other works of Bach have disappeared from the active catalog, together with her Rameau, Couperin, and others. It would be a good idea to keep an eye out for some of these recordings in the cut-out bins while awaiting their return to currency.

Joseph Szigeti

SIDE 2

Sergei Prokofiev (1891–1953)
Violin Concerto no. 1 in D major, op. 19
    I. Andantino
    II. Scherzo vivacissimo
    III. Moderato

Szigeti, violin; London Philharmonic Orchestra, Sir Thomas Beecham cond.
Recorded 23 August 1935, London. Included through the courtesy of EMI Records, Ltd.

Joseph Szigeti, who died in 1973 at the age of eighty, was another of those fabulous figures who begin life as child prodigies and continue making music on the highest level into their seventies. He was born into a musical family in Budapest, where the virtuoso-composer Jenö Hubay was one of his early teachers. At the age of twelve he made his debut in Berlin and received an offer of private lessons from the legendary Joseph Joachim; he declined that offer in favor of active concertizing and four years later introduced a concerto written for him by the Irish composer and conductor Sir Hamilton Harty. Throughout his life Szigeti, who settled in the United States in 1940 and took citizenship here in 1951, was an outstanding and authoritative performer of the widest-ranging repertoire, impeccable in Bach and Mozart, expressive in the big nineteenth-century concertos, and one of the most ardent champions of the music of his own time. His approach was at once intense and elegant, his tone pure and lean rather than lush, and his style, while always carrying a personal imprint, was remarkably adaptable to that of the music at hand. He was especially admired for his performances of the Bach sonatas and partitas for unaccompanied violin. The great Belgian violinist Eugène Ysaÿe, remembered also as a composer and conductor, was inspired by Szigeti's Bach performances to compose his own solo sonatas; he dedicated the first of them to Szigeti, of whom he wrote: "I have found in Szigeti that quality rare in our days: to be at the same time a virtuoso and a musician. One senses the artist aware of his mission—like a prophet—and one appreciates the violinist placing

Joseph Szigeti   EMI Records

technique in the service of expression.''

Szigeti's great compatriot Béla Bartók not only composed music for him (Rhapsody no. 1; *Contrasts* for clarinet, violin, and piano) but also performed as pianist with him. In 1940 they gave a recital of Beethoven, Debussy, and Bartók at the Library of Congress in Washington, and they performed and recorded the *Contrasts* with Benny Goodman. Szigeti gave the world premiere of the Bloch violin concerto in Cleveland in 1938 and made the premiere recording of it the following year; he also took up enthusiastically many contemporary works that were not written for him, though in many cases he identified himself so closely with them that they were assumed to have been. One of these was the Prokofiev concerto recorded here.

Prokofiev began work on his First Violin Concerto in 1916, but interrupted it at various points to compose his Classical Symphony and other works. He completed the orchestration in 1917 and took

83

the score with him when he left Russia for the West the following year, but five years went by before the premiere was finally given, in Paris. Serge Koussevitzky, who had established his own concert series in the French capital, introduced the concerto on 18 October 1923 with his concertmaster, Marcel Darrieux, as soloist. Bronislaw Huberman and various other violinistic luminaries had been offered the premiere, but they had all turned it down. The first major artist to play the work was Szigeti, who performed it at the International Society for Contemporary Music festival in Prague in the summer of 1924 and then played it throughout Western Europe, in Leningrad, and in London. The degree of his identification with this work is indicated in Prokofiev's autobiography:

"When [Szigeti] came to Paris and I expressed the desire to attend the rehearsal, his face fell. 'You see,' he said, 'I love that concerto and I know the score so well that I sometimes give pointers to the conductor as if it were my own composition. But you must admit that under the circumstances the presence of the author would be embarrassing for me.' I agreed and went to the concert instead. Szigeti played superbly."

It was, then, only fitting that it should be Szigeti who made the first recording of the concerto, in 1935; this was to remain the only recording of the work until after World War II. His collaborators were Sir Thomas Beecham (1879–1961) and the London Philharmonic Orchestra, with whom he also recorded Mozart's Concerto no. 4 in D (K. 218) and the Mendelssohn Concerto in E minor at about the same time. Their joint effort in the Prokofiev, preserved in this collection, was apparently Beecham's only recording of a major contemporary Russian work.

The usual fast-slow-fast sequence of the three movements of a conventional concerto is more or less reversed in this one, whose two outer movements are slowish and ruminative (though the opening one has a more animated middle section) and whose middle movement is a scherzo. Material from the first movement is recalled in the last, and the conclusion of the work virtually duplicates the end of the first movement. The whole exudes a sort of rhapsodic, fairy-tale essence, in which the biting *diablerie* of the scherzo seems the most natural sort of foil for the ethereal passages in the outer movements.

Toward the end of his life Szigeti made another recording of this concerto, but he did not have Beecham for his partner in the remake, and it had neither the pungency nor the flow nor the overall electrifying vividness of this premiere version. The historic Washington recital with Bartók (Beethoven's "Kreutzer" Sonata, the Debussy Violin Sonata, Bartók's own Sonata no. 2 and Rhapsody no. 1) is preserved in a two-disc Vanguard set, SRV-304/5. From the same period, also on Vanguard, are all the Beethoven violin sonatas, with Claudio Arrau at the piano (SRV-300/1/2/3), and a cycle of the Mozart sonatas in which George Szell is the pianist in K. 454 and K. 481 and Mieczyslaw Horszowski in all the others (SRV-262/3/4 and SRV-265/6/7). The premiere recording of Bartók's *Contrasts*, with Benny Goodman and the composer, is on Odyssey 32 16 0220; that of the Bloch Concerto, with Charles Munch and the Paris Conservatoire Orchestra, is on Turnabout THS-65007. CBS offers a six-disc collection of works by various composers in performances with various partners, some of the titles duplicating those in the other packages listed here (M6X-31513).

Alfred Cortot

SIDE 3 BAND 1

Robert Schumann (1810–1856)
Kinderszenen, op. 15

1. Of Distant Lands and People   2. A Curious Tale
3. Tag   4. Pleading Child   5. Perfect Happiness   6. Heroic
Deeds   7. Träumerei   8. By the Fireside   9. The Knight of the
Hobby Horse   10. "Almost Too Fast"   11. Throwing a
Scare   12. Slumbering Child   13. The Poet Speaks

Cortot, piano.
Recorded 4 July 1935, London. Included through the courtesy of EMI Records, Ltd.

Alfred Cortot (1877–1962) was without question the outstanding French pianist of the first half of our century, and his active career spanned that entire period and more. In contradistinction to some of the other pianists represented in this collection, Cortot was not primarily or even conspicuously a technician—in terms of sheer tech-

85

nique he was surpassed by several of his contemporaries—but his imaginativeness and profound musical understanding transcended such considerations. For the sort of thoroughgoing musicianship that distinguished a Casals or a Schnabel, Cortot had few peers. He was active at the keyboard until almost the end of his long life and, through much of it, active as conductor, teacher, editor, scholar, and all-round activist as well. As a chamber music player he formed the most celebrated of all piano trios, with violinist Jacques Thibaud and cellist Pablo Casals, and he and Thibaud also performed as a duo. As a conductor he made the very first "integral" recording of Bach's Brandenburg Concertos (with a chamber orchestra of the Ecole Normale de Musique, a school he founded in Paris in 1919) and, with Thibaud and Casals as soloists, the premiere recording of Brahms's Double Concerto (with Casals's own orchestra in Barcelona). He edited numerous works for publication, taught or coached three generations of pianists, served on prestigious juries. (As noted in the section on Dinu Lipatti, Cortot resigned from a Vienna International Competition jury in protest when Lipatti was denied first prize in 1934, and brought Lipatti to Paris to study with him.)

Before he was twenty Cortot won a reputation as a Beethoven interpreter with his performances of the concertos, and his interest in Wagner led beyond his performing two-piano arrangements of operatic excerpts to his serving as assistant conductor at Bayreuth, under the illustrious Hans Richter and Felix Mottl. At the age of twenty-four, he presided over the Paris premiere of *Götterdämmerung* and a memorable *Tristan und Isolde*. He subsequently conducted other works of Wagner and major choral works by Beethoven, Brahms, et al. His activity as a member of the Cortot-Thibaud-Casals trio and his teaching were as important to him as his solo appearances and conducting. Cortot admitted a degree of collaboration with the Nazi occupiers of France during World War II but was eventually able to effect a reconciliation with his former colleague Casals (who did not, however, allow Thibaud in his presence after the war) and continued recording into the mid-1950s.

As a pianist Cortot identified himself particularly with two great composers for his instrument, Chopin and Schumann. His line of descent from Chopin was a direct one, for one of Cortot's first teachers in Paris was Decombes, who had been Chopin's last pupil. It was not only Cortot's fondness for German culture but a long-standing affection for Schumann's music on the part of French musicians that

Alfred Cortot   *NYPL*

drew him to that composer's works. He made one of the first recordings of the Schumann Concerto, in the late 1920s, and the last of his
recordings to be issued, in 1954, was of the *Etudes symphoniques* and
Carnaval.

Schumann composed his piano suite of "Childhood Scenes" early
in 1838, and it was probably performed in the spring of that year by
Clara Wieck. On Clara's eighteenth birthday, the previous September, Schumann had written to her father to ask his blessing on their
engagement, but the elder Wieck (who had been Schumann's own
teacher for a time) did his best to block the marriage, which did not
take place until the eve of Clara's twenty-first birthday. A month
after Schumann's request for her hand, in fact, Wieck took her off on
a seven-month concert tour. In her absence Schumann produced
some of his finest works for piano—the Fantasy in C major, the
Kreisleriana (composed in only four days, according to one of his let-

87

ters), the *Novelletten,* and the *Kinderszenen.* Of the last, he wrote to Clara: "You'll enjoy it, but of course you will have to forget that you are a virtuosa."

This is not a bravura work but simple, straightforward music that might best be described as an entertainment for children in the form of reminiscences of the story-teller's childhood. In the very center of the sequence is a piece whose title is always given in German because translations such as "Dreams" or "Dreaming" or "Reverie" just don't seem to match the evocativeness of *"Träumerei"*—by which title it has become one of the most familiar of Schumann's compositions and, indeed, one of the most beloved of all musical works. At the end of the work is an epilogue in which the story-teller himself at last steps forward from behind his tales and pictures to make his personal declaration of affection.

In addition to the trios recorded with Casals, Cortot is represented now in the active domestic catalogue by his recording of the "basic fourteen" Chopin waltzes (Seraphim 60127) and by a miscellany (Seraphim 60143). His recordings of the Ravel concerto in D and the Saint-Saëns concerto in C, with Charles Munch directing the Paris Conservatoire Orchestra, are on Pathé 2C051-43370.

Léon Goossens

SIDE 3 BAND 2

Wolfgang Amadeus Mozart (1756–1791)
Oboe Quartet in F major, K. 370
    I. Allegro
    II. Adagio
    III. Rondo (Allegro)

Goossens, oboe; members of the Léner Quartet: Jëno Léner, violin; Sándor Roth, viola; Imre Hartman, cello.
Recorded 1 March 1933, London. Included through the courtesy of EMI Records, Ltd.

The oboe, one of the oldest of instruments in current use, was a mainstay in the Baroque era, when it was the most favored of all solo instruments after the violin. It is fair to say, however, that there was no internationally recognized virtuoso of the instrument until the appearance of Léon Goossens (born 1897), who changed our notions about its capacities and its very sonic textures no less dramatically than Casals did in respect to the cello. Léon is a member of the third generation of prominent English musicians in the Goossens family, both his grandfather, who came from Belgium, and his father having been conductors, as was his brother Eugène (1893–1962), who was a composer as well. His sisters Marie and Sidonie were both harpists, and a third brother, lost in World War I, played the horn. Léon became first oboe in the Queen's Hall Orchestra at sixteen and was principal in one major London orchestra or another (among them Beecham's London Philharmonic) for nearly fifty years. He gave the oboe a mellower, sweeter tone and warmer character than it had exhibited in the past, produced chiefly through his imaginative use of vibrato. His playing, in chamber music and as concerto soloist, encouraged a virtual renaissance of the oboe, and such composers as Vaughan Williams and Britten composed works for him. In 1962, at what is generally considered retirement age, Goossens had his mouth

Léon Goossens in 1980   *EMI Records*

89

virtually destroyed in an automobile accident, but after three years of surgery and rehabilitative therapy he was able to return to his career at the age of sixty-eight and to continue playing into his seventies.

Among Goossens's recordings none has been more admired than the one presented here of the Mozart Oboe Quartet, made in 1936 with members of the Léner Quartet. Possibly more than anything else on records, it served to win friends for the oboe (as well as for the work itself) and to encourage a new generation of players; for warmth of heart, vivacity, and all-round elegant style, it remains in a class by itself.

The Léner Quartet, active between the two World Wars, was made up of four Hungarian musicians who had studied together and played together in the Budapest Opera orchestra. It was the first ensemble to undertake a recording of all the Beethoven string quartets, and Eugène Goossens was one of the several composers who wrote new works for the Léners. The quartet made an affectionately remembered recording of Mozart's big Divertimento in D major, K. 334, with Aubrey Brain and his young son Dennis playing the horns, but this one of the Oboe Quartet is regarded as a high point in the Léner discography as well as that of Léon Goossens.

All of Mozart's works for solo wind instruments were written for specific players. The Oboe Quartet was composed in 1781 for Friedrich Ramm, the brilliant Mannheim oboist for whom he had composed a concerto a few years earlier. In a pastoral character suited to the oboe, this work was one of the first harbingers of the intimate chamber music style of Mozart's maturity, as well as a splendid showcase for the virtuoso oboist. The first movement is in the nature of a romantic dialogue between oboe and violin, with exquisite embellishments by the viola and cello; the second is not unlike an aria for one of the heroines in Mozart's later operas, and the finale is a rustic dance whose easygoing humor frames some thrilling display passages for the oboe.

Only one of Léon Goossens's records has survived in the U.S. catalogue; it is one he made just before his automobile accident in 1962 (Angel RL-32076), with Yehudi Menuhin and the Bath Festival Chamber Orchestra, of Bach's Concerto in D minor for violin, oboe, and strings and the three Handel oboe concertos. (On the same disc is Vivaldi's Concerto in B minor for four violins and strings, op. 3, no. 10, without Goossens.)

The Léner Quartet in 1933   *EMI Records*

Artur Schnabel

SIDE 4

Wolfgang Amadeus Mozart (1756–1791)
Piano Concerto no. 21 in C major, K. 467
    I. Allegro maestoso
    II. Andante
    III. Allegro vivace assai

Schnabel, piano; London Symphony Orchestra, Sir Malcolm Sargent cond.
Recorded January 1937, London. Included through the courtesy of EMI Records, Ltd.

Artur Schnabel (1882–1951) was born an Austrian, studied in
Vienna from age seven to eighteen, based himself in Berlin for the
next thirty-three years, and in 1939 came to the United States, where
he took citizenship five years later. One obligatory background note
on him is the one about his being told by his teacher in Vienna, the
great Theodor Leschetizky: "You will never be a pianist; you are a
musician." Another is Schnabel's own remark that he was interested
only in "music that is written better than it can be played." Early on,
Leschetizky excused him from learning the Liszt Hungarian Rhapsodies and introduced him instead to the sonatas of Schubert, which
were then all but forgotten by performers and the public alike; Schnabel took them to his heart and virtually singlehandedly brought them
out of oblivion, pronouncing them "a safe supply of happiness," and
this indicated the directions his life was to take. In Berlin he played
chamber music with cellists Casals, Fournier, and Feuermann, violists Hindemith and Primrose, and violinists Flesch, Huberman, and
Szigeti. There, too, he began his activity as a pedagogue, in which he
was to earn almost as much respect as he did as a performer, number-
ing among his pupils such pianists as Lili Kraus, Sir Clifford Curzon,
Leon Fleisher, and Claude Frank. It was also in Berlin, Schnabel
said, that he "learned how to play Beethoven."

It is with Beethoven that Schnabel's name is most strongly connected. He was regarded as the supreme authority of his time on that
master's piano works; he published his own editions of the sonatas,
and his unique position as an interpreter is well preserved on rec-

Artur Schnabel   NYPL

ords. In the early 1930s he became the first pianist to record all five
Beethoven concertos (with two London orchestras); the success of
those recordings led to his becoming the first to record all the
Beethoven sonatas, under an imaginative public subscription scheme
which was to be the forerunner of several similar projects undertaken
by EMI; the "Beethoven Sonata Society" recordings eventually
included the Diabelli Variations and several other works as well as the
sonatas. In the early 1940s Schnabel began another Beethoven concerto cycle with the Chicago Symphony Orchestra, but this project
was aborted, with only nos. 4 and 5 accounted for, when the conduc-

tor, Frederick Stock, died in 1942 and then the Musicians' Union ban on recordings went into effect. Another projected cycle after World War II, with Issay Dobrowen and the Philharmonia Orchestra, was left uncompleted because of Schnabel's own death.

In addition to Beethoven and Schubert, Schnabel played Brahms with great affection and authority (he recorded both piano concertos), and his Mozart—of which he did not record nearly enough—was also in a very special class. He was active as a composer—of works in a more or less Schoenbergian style which had no apparent relation to the music he liked to perform. In 1905 he married a German contralto, Therese Behr, whose musical outlook was similar to his own in that she specialized in lieder and eschewed the stage; Schnabel accompanied her in her recitals after they were married. One of their sons, Stefan, became a well-known actor; the other, Karl Ulrich, became an admired pianist in his own right and recorded the Mozart Two-Piano Concerto and several of Schubert's four-hand works with his father.

In many respects the most successful of all Schnabel's Mozart recordings was this exemplary one of the popular Concerto no. 21 in C major which he made in 1937 with Sir Malcolm Sargent, who had conducted in all his Beethoven concerto recordings a few years earlier. It is on a large scale, yet crystalline in all its textures, with a feeling of chamber-music give-and-take between soloist and orchestra. The recording also carries its age well.

The score of this concerto is dated 9 March 1785, less than four weeks after Mozart completed his unprecedentedly dramatic Concerto in D minor, K. 466. The contrast between the two works is itself dramatic but has its own logic. Alfred Orel observed that "the C major Concerto, with its perfectly harmonious clarity, is a natural reaction after the spiritual tempests and passionate inner battles of the D minor." Mozart wrote nothing more downright ingratiating than this very substantial concerto, which is perhaps the most "typical" of all his great Viennese keyboard concertos in that its structure adheres so thoroughly to the pattern established in those written before the D minor: a first movement in the form Alfred Einstein characterized as an "ideal march," an aria-like slow movement, and a *buffo* finale. And yet no less typical, for Mozart, is the degree of individuality that illumines this music. The exquisite slow movement earned an unexpected celebrity in the late 1960s, when it was used recurrently in a popular Swedish movie. Some record producers and concert managers even began labeling the work the *Elvira Madigan* Concerto; but the film is now remembered only for its use of this music, while the concerto of course continues to flourish without cinematic support—and on this the public may be congratulated, for, as Einstein noted, "Listeners who can really appreciate Mozart's piano concertos are the best audience there is."

Schnabel's very last recordings, made in June 1950, also happened to be Mozart concertos—the two in minor keys, no. 20 in D minor (K. 466) and no. 24 in C minor (K. 491), both with Walter Susskind conducting the Philharmonia—and are in circulation now on Turnabout THS-65046. All of Schnabel's Beethoven sonatas are available, in four Seraphim sets (ID-6063, IC-6064, IC-6065, IC-6066); the Diabelli Variations, two other sets of variations, two sets of bagatelles and several shorter works are in Seraphim IC-6067; and the five cello sonatas, with Pierre Fournier, are in Seraphim IB-6075. All five of the original Beethoven concerto recordings with Sargent are in Arabesque set 8103-4, and *all* of Schnabel's Schubert recordings—both pre-war and post-war, including not only the four-hand works with Karl Ulrich but also seven songs sung by Therese Behr-Schnabel as well as three big sonatas, the *Moments musicaux,* two sets of impromptus and several shorter solo pieces—have been collected in two sets on the same label (8137-3 and 8145-3).

Arthur Rubinstein

SIDE 5 BAND 1

Gabriel Fauré (1845–1924)
Nocturne in A-flat major, op. 33, no. 3

Rubinstein, piano.
Recorded November 1938, London. Included through the courtesy of EMI Records, Ltd.

SIDE 5 BAND 2

Francis Poulenc (1899–1963)
Mouvements perpétuels

Rubinstein, piano.
Recorded November 1938, London. Included through the courtesy of EMI Records, Ltd.

SIDE 5 BAND 3

Frédéric Chopin (1810–1849)
Three Nocturnes, op. 9

Rubinstein, piano.
Recorded February 1937 (nos. 1 & 3), October 1936 (no. 2), London. Included through the
courtesy of EMI Records, Ltd.

SIDE 5 BAND 4

Manuel de Falla (1876–1946)
Ritual Fire Dance from *El Amor brujo*

Rubinstein, piano.
Recorded 22 July 1930, London. Included through the courtesy of EMI Records, Ltd.

The stunning career of Arthur Rubinstein (1887–1982) was both
so long and so recent that there is probably very little that needs to be
said about him. He was born in Poland, lived for years in London
and Paris, traveled widely—in South America as well as Europe—
and eventually became a U.S. citizen. He signed himself Arthur once
he settled here, but his management continued to book him under his
original given name, Artur, no doubt feeling that this form evoked a
more cosmopolitan image. "Cosmopolitan" is surely the word for

96

Rubinstein—a *bon vivant* in the broadest sense, at home everywhere, picking up additions to his repertory everywhere, and giving encouragement of the most meaningful sort to countless composers. He told the story of his life himself in some detail in two entertaining books, *My Young Years* (1973) and *My Many Years* (1980), both published by Alfred A. Knopf.

The illustrious Joseph Joachim, for whom Rubinstein performed in Berlin at the age of *three,* undertook the direction of his musical training (the composer Max Bruch taught him theory) and ten years later conducted the concert in which Rubinstein made his Berlin debut, playing concertos by Mozart and Saint-Saëns and solo pieces by Schumann and Chopin. By the time he reached seventeen, Rubinstein had made his debuts in Germany, Poland, and Paris, and after that some private coaching with Paderewski in Switzerland seemed to be all he needed in the way of further instruction. His American debut was made with the Philadelphia Orchestra in New York in 1906. Unlike many other sensationally successful prodigies, Rubinstein himself not only recognized his shortcomings—a certain lack of depth and inadequate preparation of some of his material— but was able to correct them without interruption of his career or any lessening of the brilliant spontaneity and vitality that had made him a favorite everywhere. During World War I he lived in London, where he had made his debut in 1912 as accompanist to Pablo Casals; there he also served as accompanist to the great violinist Eugène Ysaÿe, and during this period he made his first visits to South America and Spain, where he came into intimate acquaintance with the music of Villa-Lobos, Albéniz, Granados, and Falla—music he did more than any other non-Spaniard to put into international circulation.

Curiously, while it is with the music of Chopin that Rubinstein was to become most closely identified, recognition for him as a Chopin player was slow in coming—largely because of his insistence on demythifying the music and replacing the sentimentalized and generally inaccurate playing that had become the expected norm with a straightforward approach and scrupulous respect for the score. "I played Chopin, so I believed, with dignity," Rubinstein recalled, "with neither sentimentality (sentiment, yes!) nor affectation, and without swooping swan-like onto the keys as pianists were wont to do as a sign to the audience that it was Chopin they were listening to." Eventually, of course, it was Rubinstein himself who was to set the standard for Chopin interpretation. But he was no less notable in the music of Beethoven, Brahms, Bach, Schumann, Schubert, Grieg, and various twentieth-century composers. His was a romantic style, but without the excesses so often identified with that term. The miracle of Rubinstein's remarkable flair for enlivening everything he played had nothing to do with the taking of liberties but everything to do with his belief in the soundness of the music and his enthusiasm for communicating it. He really did very little to call attention to himself; he focused his own attention and the audience's always and exclusively on the music.

In 1941 Rubinstein joined with Jascha Heifetz and the unforgettable cellist Emanuel Feuermann to perform and record chamber music. Feuermann's death at thirty-nine the following year brought an interruption to that activity, which was resumed in 1950 with Gregor Piatigorsky replacing him. (Rubinstein had recorded sonatas with both Heifetz and Piatigorsky in London in the mid-1930s.) Still later, Rubinstein made a number of recordings with the Guarneri Quartet. In his sixties and seventies he gave concerto cycles—series of concerts concentrated within a few weeks in which he would cover, at the rate of three works per evening, dozens of the great staples of the concerto literature. He continued performing and recording into his ninetieth year, when his failing eyesight made it difficult for him to continue. Until he stopped, he maintained his full vigor. In January 1975, the month in which he turned eighty-eight, he played the Brahms D minor Concerto and the Beethoven G major in one evening in Los Angeles, and two nights later in Pasadena gave a solo recital. Someone or something had irritated him just before the recital was to begin; he came on stage with a fiery mien and tore into the *Appassionata*. It was a performance of rare drama, passion, and sheer drive, yet with every note in place and all musical values superbly balanced. The Schumann *Fantasiestücke* (op. 12) and everything that followed sustained the heady level to the end; in the following year the Schumann and a different Beethoven sonata were the last works he recorded.

Since so much of Rubinstein's discography is in general circulation now and all the big works readily available, selections have been chosen to represent him here in some areas of the repertory in which he was uniquely authoritative and, in some cases, music whose most effective champion he was on the international circuit. Of the four composers represented, Rubinstein knew three personally and might be said to have known the fourth—Chopin—best of all.

Arthur Rubinstein   NYPL

   Gabriel Fauré composed thirteen nocturnes for piano, spread over
nearly four decades and forming the backbone of his music for piano
solo; the last of them, op. 119, composed in 1922, two years before
his death, was his final composition for the piano. Op. 33, which
began Fauré's sequence of nocturnes in 1883, is a set of three, the
only such set he composed, all of his later nocturnes being either
independent works or components of sets of pieces in diverse forms.
All of them show him as having made the nocturne a very personal
form, owing little to the examples of John Field or Chopin, and all
are intimate and poetic in nature. This concluding piece from the op.
33 set, an *Andante* in A-flat, may seem to look ahead to the piano
music of Debussy more than it echoes any earlier composer.
   Poulenc was himself a fine pianist; he performed and recorded his
concertos and chamber music with various colleagues and, with the
baritone Pierre Bernac, songs by other composers as well as his own.
He did not have a high opinion of his works for piano solo and is said

99

to have found the *Mouvements perpétuels* something of an embarrass-
ment when this set of three tiny pieces, composed in 1918, became
and remained the most popular of all his compositions for piano.
Ricardo Viñes, to whom the music was dedicated, introduced it in
the Paris concert of 5 April 1919 that gave rise to the music critic
Henri Collet's designation of the six composers represented therein
as *Les Six*. Poulenc himself made the first recording of the *Mouvements
perpétuels*, but it was Rubinstein's, and Rubinstein's frequent performances, that made the work popular. Rubinstein took up several of
Poulenc's other works, and *Les Promenades* were composed for him.

Opus numbers are not reliable guides to chronology among
Chopin's works. The three Nocturnes, op. 9, composed in 1830–31
and published in 1833, were actually preceded by two other nocturnes, one of which was given the misleading designation op. 72, no.
1, and by dozens of works in other forms bearing later opus numbers.
In any event, this set was an eloquent beginning, in the "official"
sense, for the cycle of works in which Chopin was to reach such
unprecedented levels of poetry. The second of these three nocturnes,
the one in E-flat, achieved the sort of popularity on its own that led to
its being heard in arrangements for all sorts of ensembles and as a
song with more than one set of dreadful verses fitted to it.

Manuel de Falla's ballet *El Amor brujo* was introduced in Madrid in
April 1915. A little more than a year later, on his first visit to Spain,
Rubinstein met Falla and was his guest at a performance of the ballet. Rubinstein asked the composer for his permission to arrange the
"Ritual Fire Dance" as a piano solo, and, as he recalled in *My Young
Years,* Falla gave his permission with an amused expression, doubting
that the piece would be effective. "I did arrange it," Rubinstein
wrote. "When I played it as an encore at my next concert, the public
went wild. I *had* to repeat it three times." From that time on, the
"Fire Dance" was an indispensable Rubinstein encore, and it
became a popular concert piece on its own.

Rubinstein recorded most of his repertory under prime conditions
and committed some of his specialties to records three or four times.
He was the first pianist to record all the Beethoven concertos three
times (three "integral" cycles, that is, in addition to a separate no. 3
with Toscanini and no. 4 with Beecham). His current discography
includes most of his finest recordings, and RCA now is preparing
digitally remastered editions of all of his Chopin. The nocturnes and
waltzes have already received that treatment (set ARL3-5018); so

100

have two of the trio recordings with Heifetz and Feuermann: Beethoven's *Archduke* Trio and Schubert's Trio no. 1 in B-flat, occupying one side each on RCA AGM1-5244. One hopes the Brahms op. 8 Trio will be reissued soon in this series. Among Rubinstein's other Chopin recordings, the complete Nocturnes, in RCA LSC-7050 (two discs), would make a good beginning, and several of the less frequently heard works—*Barcarolle, Berceuse, Tarantelle, Boléro, Trois Nouvelles Etudes*—are packaged with a superb performance of the *Fantaisie* in F minor on LSC-2889.

The last recordings Rubinstein made, the Beethoven Sonata in E-flat, op. 31, no. 3, and Schumann's op. 12 *Fantasiestücke,* are on RCA AGL1-4892, and the especially appealing performance of the sonata is alternatively coupled with the last of Rubinstein's three recordings of Beethoven's Second Concerto (with Daniel Barenboim conducting the London Philharmonic, ARL1-4711).

An interesting cross-section of mostly lesser-known material, brought together from live performances given in Carnegie Hall in the fall of 1961, disappeared from the domestic catalogue a few years ago but is available again on a German RCA import under the heading *In Memoriam Artur Rubinstein* (RL 42024): Prokofiev's *Visions fugitives,* Villa-Lobos's *Próle do bêbê* Suite no. 1, Four Mazurkas by Szymanowski, and four Debussy Preludes (*La cathédrale engloutie, Poissons d'or, Hommage à Rameau, Ondine*). The Brahms D minor Concerto with Reiner and the Chicago Symphony Orchestra, from a few years earlier, is outstanding, too (RCA AGL1-4890 or AGL1-5253).

Yehudi Menuhin and George Enescu

SIDE 6 BAND 1

Johann Sebastian Bach (1685–1750)
Concerto in D minor for Two Violins, BWV 1043
  I. Vivace
  II. Largo ma non tanto

Menuhin, Enescu, violins; Paris Symphony Orchestra, Pierre
Monteux cond.
Recorded 4 June 1932, Paris. Included through the courtesy of EMI Records, Ltd.

Yehudi Menuhin is the youngest of the few musicians represented in this collection who are still active today; he was also the youngest to embark on a serious career, recognized by the time he was eleven, as Boris Schwarz put it in *Great Masters of the Violin,* as "not an infant prodigy but a great artist who began at an early age." He was born in New York in 1916; his Russian Jewish immigrant parents moved to San Francisco shortly after that, and he studied there with the famous teacher Louis Persinger. He made his debut there in 1924, his New York debut two years later, and played in Paris in 1927. In his autobiography, *Unfinished Journey,* Menuhin recalls that when he was seven or eight Enescu came to San Francisco to conduct one of his symphonies and play the Brahms Concerto: "Before a note was sounded he had me in thrall. His countenance, his stance, his wonderful mane of black hair—everything about him proclaimed the free man, the man who is strong with the freedom of gypsies, of spontaneity, of creative genius, of fire." When the ten-year-old Menuhin first went to Europe, Persinger sent him to play for Eugène Ysaÿe in Brussels, but it was only Enescu he wanted to teach him, and in Paris he simply went to Enescu's house, as the latter was preparing to leave on a tour, and demanded—and got—his first lesson.

Enescu (1881–1955), remembered chiefly as a composer now (but only for his Rumanian Rhapsodies, his more ambitious works being heard only rarely), was himself an outstanding violinist, a fine pianist, and a respected conductor. He was not a pedagogue in the sense

102

Enescu with the young Menuhin   NYPL

that Joachim and Schnabel were, but he is remembered perhaps as much for being Menuhin's teacher as for his other distinctions, and he subsequently taught Arthur Grumiaux, Christian Ferras, and a number of other violinists. Menuhin wrote: "Having started at the age of five, within no time Enescu played the violin expertly. The superb quality of his trills, vibrato, bowing, he must have had from the beginning, discovering them in himself with no more recourse to theory than the Gypsies had . . . If his innate powers were cultivated in the rigorous classical schools of Vienna and Paris, the schooling in no way dampened their force, nor fastened them down to any man's technical directives. He remained himself. When I came to study with him, I too played more or less as a bird sings, instinctively, uncalculatingly, unthinkingly, and thus neither he nor I gave much thought to theory."

It is a mark of Enescu's commitment to his charge that after a time he sent Menuhin to Adolf Busch, who with his utterly different approach instilled in him the standards of the German tradition. (Busch's brother Fritz conducted Menuhin's New York orchestral debut in the Beethoven Violin Concerto in November 1927, the performance that made him an international figure.) Menuhin and Enescu remained close to the end of the latter's life, and in the 1930s they recorded together, with Enescu in all three of his roles as performer: he was the pianist in his own Third Violin Sonata, he conducted for Menuhin in concertos by Mozart and Dvořák, and in the Bach Double Concerto, heard here, he was his violin partner, with their friend the great Pierre Monteux conducting.

Menuhin's early mastery showed a rare balance of technique and spontaneity, and neither of these qualities abandoned him as his insights deepened over the years, though in his thirties he made an effort to clarify for himself the specific processes involved in what he now describes as "instinctive" and "unthinking." His enormous repertoire includes works written for him by such composers as Bartók, Bloch, and Frank Martin, and he has performed and recorded as violist in the last two decades. He became seriously involved with teaching as well as with Indian music, international human rights,

Yehudi Menuhin   NYPL

George Enescu   NYPL

and other causes. After World War II he visited Europe to perform in displaced persons camps as well as concert halls, and showed great moral courage in speaking up in defense of the conductor Wilhelm Furtwängler, who was then under a bit of a cloud for having remained in Nazi Germany through World War II, and with whom he recorded the Bartók Concerto no. 2 as well as concertos of Beethoven, Brahms, and Mendelssohn. Menuhin himself eventually became a conductor, presiding over his own festivals in Britain and appearing now with many of the world's orchestras in that capacity. He has written several books and recently presented a television series called *The Music of Man.* His late sister Hephzibah performed and recorded with him frequently as pianist; his other sister, Yaltah, is also a pianist, as is his son Jeremy.

No musician has been more beloved than Enescu, by his colleagues, the international public, or his compatriots. (The original Rumanian form of his name is just coming into international usage now, the gallicized "Georges Enesco" having been used by Enescu himself in his international touring.) His Rumanian Poem for orchestra was performed in Paris when he was only sixteen; he conducted the premier of his two Rumanian Rhapsodies in Bucharest in 1903.

105

His status as a national figure is confirmed everywhere: the city of his birth was renamed George Enescu, and the leading Rumanian orchestra and conservatory bear his name, as do streets, monuments, and competitions. At the age of ten he played violin in the Vienna Konservatorium Orchestra in performances conducted by Brahms and began developing his career as violinist together with his composing at a very early age. He is on record as having chosen to make "some concessions to technical perfection" in order both to build up a huge repertory (in a single winter series in Bucharest he played sixty different sonatas) and, more important, "that my interpretations can evolve, free from any threat of mechanization. There are, after all, several valid ways of interpreting any piece of music."

Enescu earned special respect for his performances of Bach's violin works, which he recorded; Menuhin also became closely identified with Bach (eventually as conductor as well as violinist and violist), and it is in Bach's sole concerto for two violins that the two made their only recording together as violinists.

Bach composed this concerto at Cöthen in 1720. It was in that happy environment that he composed the bulk of his concert music—the Brandenburg Concertos, two of the orchestral suites, the works for unaccompanied cello and violin, and nearly all his concertos in their original form. He had composed the first of his violin concertos at Weimar before coming to Cöthen in 1717, and he composed one or two original keyboard concertos in Leipzig in 1730, but all the other keyboard concertos he produced there are essentially transcriptions of his earlier concertos for violin, those without identifiable models presumably adapted from originals lost during his lifetime. The Concerto for Two Violins was transcribed in this manner sometime between 1730 and 1736 to become the Concerto in C minor for Two Harpsichords identified as BWV 1062.

The robust concertos of Vivaldi, which Bach admired enough to transcribe several of them for solo harpsichord or solo organ or as keyboard concertos, surely served as a collective model for this inspiriting double concerto. Within its concise structure, though, one finds an expansiveness and a degree of adventurousness, even beyond Vivaldi's, that mark it as one of Bach's most forward-looking compositions. The strong themes and energetic drama of the two outer movements, the still Italianate singing line of the slow movement, and the rich and varied coloring Bach achieves with the simplest of means combine to make this concerto at once one of the most directly appealing and most rewarding of his works in this format.

Although Menuhin played the Tchaikovsky Violin Concerto in his boyhood, it remains the one important concerto he has never recorded. He has done some of the others, the Bartók among them, as many as four times. His splendid recordings of the Bloch Concerto, the Walton concertos for violin and for viola, and the Bartók Viola Concerto have all disappeared from the current catalogue, but his adventurousness is represented on cassette in his Furtwängler/ Philharmonia performance of the Bartók Violin Concerto no. 1 (Pantheon 951). Mendelssohn's early Violin Concerto in D minor for Strings was actually discovered by Menuhin and edited for publication by him in 1952; he performs it and the big Mendelssohn Concerto in E minor with the London Symphony Orchestra under Rafael Frühbeck de Burgos on Angel RL-32102. Further adventurousness is represented by his recordings of Indian music with the sitar player Ravi Shankar (Angel S-36026 and S-36418) and with the jazz violinist Stéphane Grappelli (Angel S-36968 and S-37156). The two spurious Mozart concertos in D major—the so-called *Adélaïde* actually composed by Marius Casadesus and the one listed as K. 271a—are played and conducted by Menuhin with his Bath Festival Orchestra on Angel RL-32015, as are the genuine Mozart nos. 3 and 5 on RL-32000. Of his several recordings of the Beethoven and Brahms concertos, the most valuable are those he made with Furtwängler: the second of their two recordings of the Beethoven, made with the Philharmonia Orchestra in 1953, is on Seraphim 60135, with Beethoven's Romance in G, op. 40; their Brahms, taped with the Lucerne Festival Orchestra in 1949, was on 60232 (now out of print), together with the Beethoven Romance op. 50 from the 1953 sessions.

Enescu can be heard as pianist in the Adagio and Fugue from his Suite no. 1, op. 3, and as violinist in his Sonatas nos. 2 (op. 6) and 3 ("In Rumanian Folk Style," op. 25), with Dinu Lipatti as his pianist, in Musical Heritage Society set 7025/26 (with compositions by Lipatti). The same performance of the op. 6 Sonata is paired with Enescu's String Quartet op. 22, no. 2, played by the Romanian Quartet, on Monitor MC 2049, and a different one, in which Enescu is accompanied by Céline Chaillez-Richez, is on Varese-Sarabande VC 81048. On that label Enescu is also represented as conductor, with the Colonne Orchestra in the two Rumanian Rhapsodies and with wind soloists of the Orchestre National in his *Dixtuor*, op. 14 (VC 81042).

107

Dinu Lipatti

SIDE 6 BAND 2

Frédéric Chopin (1810–1849)
Waltz in C-sharp minor, op. 64, no. 2
Waltz in A-flat major, op. 64, no. 3
Waltz in F minor, op. 70, no. 2
Waltz in D-flat major, op. 70. no. 3
Grande Valse brillante in E-flat major, op. 18

Lipatti, piano.

Recorded July 1950, Geneva. Included through the courtesy of EMI Records, Ltd.

Dinu Lipatti (1917–1950), one year younger than Menuhin, was another musician profoundly influenced by Enescu—who was in fact his godfather. (Lipatti gained a further family connection with Enescu when he married the pianist and teacher Madeleine Cantacuzène, Enescu's stepdaughter.) Lipatti, whose name Dinu is actually the diminutive of his baptismal name, Constantin, was born to a mother who played the piano well and a father who had studied violin with both Pablo de Sarasate and Carl Flesch. Like both Menuhin and Enescu, he showed his talent early: at four he was both playing and composing, and he was sent to the renowned teacher Flora Musicescu, with whom he studied for several years. In his teens he won numerous prizes as both pianist and composer. When he won only second prize in the Vienna (piano) Competition of 1934, Alfred Cortot expressed his indignation by resigning from the jury and inviting Lipatti to coach with him in Paris. There Lipatti pursued his study of composition with Paul Dukas and Nadia Boulanger and studied conducting with Charles Munch.

By the time he reached twenty he was known and admired throughout Europe; in 1943 he and his wife made their way from Bucharest to Geneva, where he lived till his death seven years later. Lipatti's health was delicate all his life, causing him to be excused from school attendance as a boy and later, when leukemia was diagnosed, to cancel tours that would have taken him to America and

Dinu Lipatti   NYPL

Australia. Munch, Menuhin, Stravinsky, and other musicians helped to cover the cost of his medical treatment, but all the efforts were to prove futile, and he died at the early age of thirty-three. As Lipatti withdrew more and more from public appearances, he came to value the opportunity to make recordings, and the few he left all show the blend of subtlety, vitality, clarity, and deep reserves of spiritual power that made his art the special thing it was. His last public recital, given at Besançon ten weeks before his death, was recorded live, preserving evidence that his unique commitment and integrity were in full force to the very end.

Lipatti performed Chopin's waltzes frequently, presenting the "basic" fourteen in a sequence of his own which was neither chronological nor determined by opus number groupings, but was devised in terms of musical continuity. He began and ended with the last and first, respectively, of the three *Valses brillantes* that constitute op. 34, and the second member of that group was placed a little past the middle of the sequence. We hear none of these in the selection included here, which does, however, end with the only other work Chopin designated a *valse brillante.* Our handful begins with the voluptuously insinuating Waltz in C-sharp minor, op. 64, no. 2, a piece vaguely tinged with melancholy and not at all vague in its nocturnal character. The three waltzes of op. 64 were actually composed as a set, in 1846 and '47, and published in the latter year. The first of them is the familiar *Minute* Waltz in D-flat, not included here; the last, which follows the C-sharp minor here, is in A-flat, the most prominent key among all Chopin's waltzes. Exactly 100 years after its publication, Arthur Hedley remarked on the "discreet, suave elegance and . . . harmonic interest" of this particular A-flat waltz, noting that "the dance element disappears altogether in the C major trio with its broad cello [-like] melody." Op. 70 was a posthumously published collection, representing both ends of Chopin's creative life: its no. 2, in F minor, was actually a fairly late work, composed in 1841, but no. 3, in D-flat, was composed in 1829, before he left Warsaw. The *Grande Valse brillante* in E-flat, op. 18, was the first of Chopin's waltzes to be published, in 1831; it is one of the three waltzes used in the ballet to his music called *Les Sylphides,* wherein it constitutes the finale, and it was cited by Hedley as a good example of Chopin's characteristic layout in this form: "a suite of sixteen-bar waltz movements in contrasting character, purely rhythmic, coquettish or ardently sentimental, leading to a coda in which the excitement of the dance comes to a head."

The valedictory recital at Besançon was long available in a two-disc Angel set, B-3556. It contained two Schubert impromptus, thirteen Chopin waltzes, Mozart's Sonata no. 8 in A minor, K. 310, and Bach's Partita no. 1 in B-flat. Several of these titles, recorded earlier, are still available, on Odyssey: the Bach and Mozart on 32 16 0320, together with four Bach transcriptions (among them Myra Hess's arrangement of "Jesu, Joy of Man's Desiring" and two chorales transcribed by Busoni). All fourteen Chopin waltzes, including the performances presented here, are on 32 16 0058. A recording of Chopin's E minor Concerto once attributed to Lipatti turned out to be by someone else (Halina Czerny-Stefanska), but there is more of Lipatti's Chopin—the Third Sonata, the *Barcarolle,* a nocturne and a mazurka—on Odyssey 32 16 0369, and still more on Turnabout THS-34832—another nocturne and two etudes, together with Bach's

Concerto in D minor, with Eduard van Beinum conducting the Concertgebouw Orchestra. A four-disc Angel set labeled *The Art of Dinu Lipatti* (ZD-3924) *does* include a Lipatti performance of the Chopin concerto, as well as the Besançon material, the Mozart concerto, the Chopin pieces that are on Odyssey 32 16 0369, the Enescu Third Sonata, and two solo items unavailable elsewhere: Liszt's *Sonetto del Petrarca 104* and a particularly stunning performance of Ravel's *Alborada del gracioso.*

In addition to the recordings with Enescu listed in the preceding section, it should be noted that the MHS set also includes Lipatti's performances of his own Sonatine for the Left Hand and his Concertino in Classic Style, the latter with Hans von Benda conducting the Berlin Chamber Orchestra.

Emanuel Feuermann

SIDE 7 BAND 1

Ernest Bloch (1880–1959)
Schelomo

Feuermann, cello; Philadelphia Orchestra, Leopold Stokowski cond.
Recorded March 1940, Philadelphia. Included through the courtesy of RCA Records.

Emanuel Feuermann was one of several outstanding musicians born on St. Cecilia's Day (Cecilia being the patron saint of music), in his case on 22 November 1902 in Austrian Galicia. Although he died without completing his fortieth year (25 May 1942 in New York), he was active with distinction for more than twenty years, in which time he earned a reputation as one of the greatest performing artists of his time and perhaps the greatest of all masters of his noble instrument, the cello. He made recordings with the most distinguished of partners, in both chamber music and orchestral works, which pointedly illustrate why so many, in Irving Kolodin's words, "esteem him still as a paragon of taste, tone, and technique."

Feuermann began serious study in Vienna before he was seven years old and made his debut three years later with Felix Weingartner and the Vienna Philharmonic Orchestra. At sixteen he was teaching at the Leipzig Conservatory; he subsequently held a professorship at the Hochschule für Musik in Berlin and first chair in the Gurzenich Orchestra of Cologne, and he formed a string trio with the violinist Szymon Goldberg and the composer-violist Paul Hindemith. Feuermann left Germany in 1933, performed in Japan as well as throughout Europe, made his U.S. debut with Bruno Walter and the New York Philharmonic in 1935, and settled here in 1938. By that time he had made his celebrated recordings of the Beethoven A major Sonata (with Myra Hess), Schubert's *Arpeggione* Sonata, and the Haydn D major Concerto. In the U.S. he began recording concerted works with the Philadelphia Orchestra under both Eugene Ormandy and Leopold Stokowski and a series of chamber music recordings with Jascha Heifetz, Arthur Rubinstein, and William Primrose. He made the premiere recording of Bloch's *Schelomo* with Stokowski in 1940, and for years, both in its original form on 78s and in various short-lived LP reissues, it was a prime collector's item—a performance filled with passion, drama, and vivid colors, yet in every bar upholding the exceptional standards cited in Kolodin's alliterative reference.

Ernest Bloch, who was born Swiss and died an American, celebrated both his native and adopted countries in his music, but he is especially remembered, in terms of ethnic identity, as a composer of "Jewish music," in forms ranging from the choral *Israel Symphony* and a setting of the *Sacred Service* for the Sabbath to the *Three Jewish Poems* for orchestra and the *Suite hébraique* and *Baal Shem* for violin and piano. *Schelomo* is outstanding in Bloch's "Jewish cycle." The title is the Hebrew form of the name Solomon, and Bloch took his inspiration from the Book of Ecclesiastes, the authorship of which has been attributed to King Solomon.

Bloch wrote of this work: "One may imagine that the voice of the cello is the voice of King Solomon. The complex voice of the orchestra is the voice of his age, his world, his experience. There are times when the orchestra seems to reflect his thoughts, just as the solo cello voices his words." The work in its several interlinked episodes depicts Solomon ruminating on his power and possessions within the framework of the lamentation, "Vanity of vanities, all is vanity!" *Schelomo* was composed in 1916 for the cellist Alexander Barjansky, but in the premiere, given in New York on 13 May 1917 with Bloch conducting, the soloist was Hans Kindler, whom Stokowski brought from Holland to be first cellist of the Philadelphia Orchestra and who subsequently

112

Emanuel Feuermann   NYPL

became the founding conductor of the National Symphony Orchestra in Washington.

Feuermann recorded the Dvořák Concerto in Berlin, but that recording never reached our shores in regular distribution. (It is now available as an import, Opal 809.) His recordings of the Haydn Cello Concerto with Sir Malcolm Sargent and of Strauss's *Don Quixote* with Ormandy are not around now, nor are the marvelous recordings of solo works he made in New York with Franz Rupp as his pianist, but the high points of his European recording activity, the Beethoven A major Sonata (op. 69) with Myra Hess at the piano and Schubert's *Arpeggione* Sonata with Gerald Moore (with whom Feuermann fills out the side in a Weber *Andantino*), are available readily and economically on Seraphim 60117.

All the recordings made with Heifetz are back in circulation now, too. The stunning account of Dohnányi's Serenade in C for string trio, with Primrose, has been reissued on RCA ARM-4942 (with Heifetz's performance of the Gruenberg Violin Concerto). The same

113

trio's performance of Mozart's Divertimento in E-flat, K. 563, is the opening item in the six-record *Heifetz Chamber Music Collection* (CRM6-2264), and the towering one of the Brahms Double Concerto, with Heifetz and Ormandy, is in Volume IV of RCA's *Heifetz Collection* series (ARM4-0495). The recordings of piano trios with Heifetz and Rubinstein are listed in the Rubinstein section above.

Gregor Piatigorsky and Solomon

SIDE 7 BAND 2

Ludwig van Beethoven (1770–1827)
Sonata for Cello and Piano, op. 102, no. 1
      I. Andante—Allegro vivace
     II. Adagio—Tempo d'andante—Allegro vivace

Piatigorsky, cello; Solomon, piano.
Recorded 8 October 1954, London. Included through the courtesy of EMI Records, Ltd.

    Gregor Piatigorsky (1903–1976) liked to describe himself as "not the greatest cellist, just the tallest." He was indeed tall and strikingly handsome, and his career spanned some six decades. He took up the cello at the age of seven in his Russian home town, entered the Moscow Conservatory on a scholarship at nine, and at sixteen became both the cellist of the Lenin Quartet and principal cellist of the Bolshoi Theater Orchestra. In 1921, by then all of eighteen, he left Russia for further study with Julius Klengel in Leipzig, and three years later Furtwangler signed him on as first cellist of the Berlin Philharmonic. In 1928 Piatigorsky gave up his orchestra position to strike out on a solo career. In Berlin he played sonatas and trios with Artur Schnabel and Carl Flesch, and there he met Nathan Milstein and Vladimir Horowitz, with whom he came to the United States. He made his American debut with the New York Philharmonic in 1929.
    Even in the years in which Casals and Feuermann were active, Piatigorsky was recognized as a master, and several important works were composed for him, among them the cello concertos of Hindemith and Walton. Strauss expressed particular pleasure in Piati-

gorsky's way with his *Don Quixote* (which the cellist recorded twice). Piatigorsky composed some music for his instrument and arranged several works by composers of various periods. He celebrated his seventieth birthday in several concerts in 1973 and continued performing on both sides of the Atlantic until his last years. After directing chamber music activities at the Berkshire Music Center (Tanglewood), he taught at the University of Southern California for the twenty-four years preceding his death. Boris Schwarz wrote of Piatigorsky's "combining an innate flair for virtuosity with an exquisite taste in style and phrasing; technical perfection was never a goal in itself. His vibrant tone had infinite shadings and his sweeping eloquence and aristocratic grandeur created an instant rapport with his audience."

Piatigorsky never recorded trios with Milstein and Horowitz, though he did make a recording of the Brahms Double Concerto with Milstein (and a second with Heifetz). He did, however, have some distinguished chamber music partners in recordings before he teamed up with Heifetz and Rubinstein; in addition to those already noted, there were Schnabel, with whom he recorded a single Beethoven sonata in the 1930s, and the superb English pianist Solomon, with whom he recorded all of Beethoven's sonatas for cello and piano in

Solomon   *EMI Records*

Gregor Piatigorsky   *EMI Records (Fox Photos)*

115

the early fifties. The English label HMV (part of the EMI combine) and the U.S. firm RCA (then known as RCA Victor) terminated their long-standing transatlantic affiliation shortly after these recordings were issued, and the set never turned up again in general circulation. (The U.S. release included Beethoven's sets of variations for cello and piano as well as the sonatas, but in the variations Piatigorsky's keyboard partner was Lukas Foss, not Solomon.)

Solomon, one year older than Piatigorsky, also had an early start. He was born in London in 1902 and made his debut at the age of eight in Mozart's B-flat Concerto and the slow movement of the big Tchaikovsky Concerto. (His family name is Cutner, but as a child he decided to use his given name alone, and that was to remain his professional name throughout his career.) Within a year he was touring as a soloist, performing concertos with major conductors, playing chamber music with distinguished senior instrumentalists. When he was fifteen Solomon decided to withdraw from public activity on the advice of the conductor Sir Henry Wood, in order to re-evaluate and redirect his career; his return three years later showed that he had made an unusually thorough and successful transition from child prodigy to mature artist.

It must be said, though, that Solomon's artistry was never less than mature; even in the year of his debut, when his feet reached the pedals only with great effort, it was the depth of his musicianship as much as his marvelous technical skill that astounded musicians everywhere. That force of his exceptional musical intellect kept Solomon from ever exploiting his technique for the sake of mere show; instead, he placed all of his formidable gifts self-effacingly at the service of the music he continued to explore, to discover, to communicate. The late conductor Walter Susskind, who made a recording or two with Solomon, once recalled that when he lived across the street from him in London he would often hear him practicing—not only *before* a major performance but *afterward*. "He would come home after giving a recital," Susskind said, "and spend hours going over the works he had just performed—always less than satisfied, always driven to bring himself nearer to perfection." Just at the time Solomon had brought himself nearest to that elusive goal, he was felled by a stroke, in 1956, which left him unable to continue performing; for nearly three full decades one of the greatest of all pianists has endured an enforced silence, with only his recordings to speak for him.

As the foregoing remarks would suggest, it was with works on the very highest level of keyboard music that Solomon chose to identify himself. He was a superb Mozart player; his Beethoven was majestic without posturing, his Schumann, Chopin, Brahms, and Debussy touched by true poetry. His recordings of the two Brahms concertos, the B-flat in particular, show him as a peerless master at balancing the power and grace, the subtlety and brilliance that are all characteristics of these complex, large-scale works, with the same apparent ease and spontaneity with which he balanced the dignity and enlivenment that were the twin hallmarks of his style. He brought the same qualities to his performances of Tchaikovsky, Liszt, and contemporary works. He was making his way through a complete recorded cycle of the Beethoven piano sonatas when he was put out of action; he had, fortunately, completed the concertos and the set of cello sonatas with Piatigorsky from which the present recording was taken.

Beethoven's five sonatas for piano and cello appeared in three installments, each more or less initiating one of the three periods of his creative life. The first pair (op. 5, 1796) was dedicated to King Friedrich Wilhelm II of Prussia, and the glorious op. 69 in A major (1808) to the Baron von Gleichenstein; both of those noble dedicatees were accomplished cellists who were expected to perform the respective works. The final pair (op. 102) was composed for a professional cellist whose name does not appear in a dedication. In 1815 the destruction of Count Rasumovsky's palace caused the suspension of his chamber music programs, and the members of his personally maintained string quartet took a long holiday before reassembling on their own as the Schuppanzigh Quartet (the ensemble that introduced most of Beethoven's subsequent quartets and many of Schubert's). During that hiatus the group's cellist, Joseph Linke, went to Croatia with the family of the Hungarian Count Peter Erdody, with whom Beethoven was on especially cordial terms: he not only wrote his final pair of cello sonatas specifically for Linke to play for the Erdodys but dedicated the last one to the Countess, to whom he wrote letters filled with puns on the cellist's name.

The music, however, is not jocular. Both of the op. 102 sonatas are challenging and superbly organized works without an ounce of fat on them, probing depths to be sounded further in the final piano sonatas and string quartets yet to come. The Sonata no. 1 in C major, the shortest in Beethoven's series of five for these instruments, is laid out in only two movements, the first of which is a conventional sonata *Allegro* with a slow introduction. The second movement is in three distinct sections, the ruminative middle one embodying reminiscences of the opening *Andante;* the mood is broken by the sparkling *Allegro vivace* which concludes the work, though it too is interrupted for occasional backward glances.

Piatigorsky's recording of the Beethoven Sonata in G minor, op. 5, no. 2, with Schnabel, is available on Seraphim 60300, together with his Brahms Sonata in E minor, op. 38, with Rubinstein. He subsequently recorded both of the Brahms sonatas (opp. 38 and 99) with Rubinstein in stereo (RCA ARL1-2085). A delayed release from the Heifetz-Piatigorsky series brings the Brahms String Quintet no. 2 in G major (op. 111) and Beethoven's Piano Trio in E-flat (op. 70, no. 2), with such associates as Leonard Pennario, piano, Israel Baker, violin, and the violists Milton Thomas and Paul Rosenthal (Vox Cum Laude VCL-9041). From the RCA series, the Beethoven String Trio op. 9, no. 2, Schubert's String Trio no. 2, and two Bach *sinfonie,* all with Heifetz and Primrose, have been reissued on RCA AGL1-4947, and there are works for violin and cello by Stravinsky (Piatigorsky's composer-approved adaptation of the *Suite italienne* derived from *Pulcinella*), Glière, and Handel (the Halvorsen-arranged Passacaglia) on CBS M 33447. Still more chamber music is in the six-disc Heifetz chamber music set listed in the Heifetz section of this booklet.

Little orchestral material remains available, but what there is is treasurable. Both of Piatigorsky's recordings of the Brahms Double Concerto (one with Heifetz, Ormandy conducting; the other with Milstein, Reiner conducting) are gone, as are his two of Strauss's *Don Quixote* (one with Reiner, one with Munch) and his two of the Saint-Saëns A-minor Concerto (one with Stock, one with Reiner). What we do have are magnificent stereophonic recordings of the Walton Concerto (dedicated to him) and Bloch's *Schelomo* on one RCA Gold Seal disc (AGL1-4086), and his similarly impressive account of the great Dvořák Concerto in B minor on the same label (AGL1-5265). All three of these are with Charles Munch and the Boston Symphony Orchestra; the Dvořák has been remastered digitally.

Solomon's recordings of the two Brahms Concertos, both with the Philharmonia, are on Turnabout now; Rafael Kubelik conducts in no. 1 (THS-65110), Issay Dobrowen in the especially grand account of no. 2 (THS-65071). With the Philharmonia Orchestra under Dobrowen and Walter Susskind, respectively, Solomon can be heard on Turnabout THS-65108 in Tchaikovsky's Concerto no. 1 and Liszt's *Hungarian Fantasia,* both of which works were prominent in his repertory from the beginning of his career, and both of which gain substance in his hands with no sacrifice of their innate excitement. Solomon made a few recordings in stereo just before he suffered his stroke; among these were splendid performances of the Grieg and Schumann concertos and Beethoven's nos. 1 and 3—all deleted now. A two-disc EMI set (RLS 726) in which Solomon plays three Mozart concertos (with the Philharmonia under Otto Ackermann in no. 15 and Herbert Menges in nos. 23 and 24) and two sonatas (K. 331 in A, K. 576 in D) may still be available as an import. Also available are several of the Beethoven sonatas he recorded in the projected cycle that had to be abandoned in 1956: the *Pathétique, Moonlight* and *Appassionata* are on Seraphim 60286; the *Waldstein* and the five late sonatas are in Turnabout set THS-65068/70.

William Primrose and William Kapell

SIDE 8 BAND 1

Johannes Brahms (1833–1897)
Viola Sonata, op. 120, no. 1
    I. Allegro appassionato
    II. Andante un poco adagio
    III. Allegretto grazioso
    IV. Vivace

Primrose, viola; Kapell, piano.
Recorded 7 May 1946, New York. Included through the courtesy of RCA Records.

Few performers select the viola initially as their instrument, and William Primrose (1903–1983) was no exception. He began his studies in his native Glasgow with the intention of becoming a violinist, and it was not until his early twenties that he changed to the viola on the advice of Eugène Ysaÿe, with whom he studied in Brussels from 1925 to 1927. He quickly found his niche, as both a touring soloist and a member of the London String Quartet. When the NBC Symphony Orchestra was created for Toscanini in 1937 Primrose was its principal violist, and he remained in the orchestra for five years, dur-

William Primrose   *EMI Records (James Abresch)*

ing which he also organized his own string quartet, the Primrose Quartet. By then he was acknowledged as being without peer among violists. The composer Paul Hindemith had achieved recognition as a violist (performing on the viola d'amore as well), and in Britain the fine violists Lionel Tertis and Frederick Riddle earned a great deal of respect for the instrument, but it was left to Primrose to raise the viola to the level of a virtuoso solo instrument in the same sense as the violin or cello. Several composers wrote music for him; one of them was Béla Bartók, whose very last work was the Viola Concerto commissioned by Primrose. Once Primrose established the viola, other performers arose to carry on and expand the repertory, and such violinists as Yehudi Menuhin, Josef Suk, David Oistrakh, and Pinchas Zukerman took up the viola in addition to the violin. All four, in fact, have recorded the solo part in Berlioz's "symphony with viola obbligato," *Harold in Italy.*

It was Primrose, appropriately, who made the first recording of *Harold in Italy,* and he recorded most of the instrument's major literature—some titles (*Harold* among them) as many as three times. Even

120

more appropriately, it was Primrose who made the premiere recording of the concerto Bartók composed for him; that work had to be put together after Bartók's death by his friend and associate Tibor Serly, who conducted in the recording (Bartók 309), issued by the Bartók Record Society operated by the composer's son Peter.

In 1941, when Heifetz, Feuermann, and Rubinstein began recording chamber music together, Primrose joined the two string players to record some of the great works for two and three strings, and he later continued the series with Heifetz and Piatigorsky. Among concerted works, he recorded Mozart's *Sinfonia concertante* three times, the last with Heifetz, with whom he also recorded Arthur Benjamin's *Romantic Fantasy.* In 1962 he joined Heifetz and Piatigorsky in teaching master classes at the University of Southern California, and subsequently taught at Indiana University and in Japan. He published a book of memoirs, *Walk on the North Side,* in 1978.

The two sonatas (op. 120) that Brahms composed originally for clarinet and piano are basic to the viola literature, and Primrose recorded each of them twice. His mid-1950s monophonic recording of the pair with Rudolf Firkušný as his keyboard partner is still in the current catalogue (Seraphim 60011). His pre-war account of no. 2 with Gerald Moore circulated for some time, and the recording of

William Kapell   *International Piano Archives at Maryland*

no. 1 which he made shortly after World War II with the lamented William Kapell is the one by which he is represented in this collection.

The tragic death of William Kapell in an airplane crash near San Francisco, on his way home from an Australian tour, in October 1953 brought to a premature end one of the most exciting careers in American music. Kapell, then just a month past his thirty-first birthday, had been one of the several remarkable pupils of Olga Samaroff and had won both the Philadelphia Orchestra Youth Competition and the Naumburg Award in 1941; in consequence of his Naumburg-sponsored New York debut in October of that year he received the Town Hall Award for the finest recital of the year by a musician under the age of thirty. At the end of the war the music of Khachaturian was discovered by American audiences, and Kapell became especially identified with that composer's Piano Concerto, which he performed throughout the country with enormous success and recorded with Koussevitzky in Boston. He presented a memorable account of the Rachmaninoff Third Concerto in Chicago, and his interpretive sympathies extended to the entire Classical and Romantic repertory as well as the most substantial contemporary works. In whatever he undertook to play, he showed a remarkable combination of interpretive insight, technical command, and sheer communicative power. In addition to a handful of concerted works and a few solo items, Kapell recorded sonatas—both by Brahms, as it happened—with two of the outstanding string players of his time, Heifetz and Primrose. With Heifetz he recorded the Sonata in D minor, op. 108, in November 1950; this was originally issued on LP, and is in fact available now in volume 6 of RCA's *Heifetz Collection* (ARM4-0947). Kapell's recording of the op. 120, no. 1, Sonata was made earlier and issued only on 78s by RCA Victor; it appears here on LP for the first time.

Toward the end of his life, Brahms followed Mozart's example (by almost exactly a hundred years) in becoming enamored of the clarinet through the artistry of an outstanding virtuoso. In Mozart's case it was Anton Stadler, for whom he composed the Trio, K. 498, the Quintet, K. 581, and the last of his concertos for any instrument, K. 622. In Brahms's case it was Richard Mühlfeld, the principal clarinetist of the famous Meiningen Orchestra, for whom he, as Mozart had done, composed both a trio (op. 114) and a quintet (op. 115), but instead of a final concerto he produced his last works in the realm of chamber music, a pair of sonatas "for piano and Mühlfeld" (op.

120). When Brahms completed these sonatas, in 1894, he declared that no other clarinetist but Mühlfeld should play them, and may actually have felt that no other clarinetist would have been able to do them justice. Whether for that reason or simply to increase the smallish repertory of the viola, he transcribed both of the sonatas for the viola, and for the violin as well. The violin versions are hardly ever performed, but the sonatas have become cornerstones of the viola repertory as well as that of the clarinet. Both of the sonatas are contemplative, "autumnal" works, but they are not without vigor; the slow movement indeed has a nostalgic character and also carries reminders of Brahms's love for the classics, but the opening movement of the F minor is a passionate episode, combining elements of Brahms's beloved variation style with those of sonata form. The trio of the third-movement *Allegretto grazioso,* too, is vigorous and colorful, and the final *Vivace,* in F major, is charged with virtuosic feeling.

Among Primrose's surviving recordings, the second, and musically the finest, of his three of Berlioz's *Harold in Italy,* the one with Sir Thomas Beecham and the Royal Philharmonic, carries its years well on Odyssey Y-33286. Two of his three of the Mozart *Sinfonia concertante* are available, and both are worth hearing: with Isaac Stern, violin, and Pablo Casals, conductor, in the five-disc set of material from the Prades and Perpignan festivals (CBS M5X-32768), and in stereo with Heifetz, Izler Solomon conducting (RCA AGL1-4929).

It was in Mozart's music that Primrose made some of his finest chamber music recordings. He recorded two of the string quintets with Heifetz, Piatigorsky, et al. on RCA, and all six of them with the Griller Quartet for Vanguard, but the gems are of pre-war vintage: the second of the two duos for violin and viola (B-flat, K. 424), with Heifetz alone, and the great Divertimento in E-flat (K. 563), with Heifetz and Feuermann. Both performances are in the *Heifetz Chamber Music Collection* (RCA set CRM6-2264), as is the Heifetz/Primrose recording of the Handel/Halvorsen Passacaglia. A perhaps even more treasurable chamber music recording from the same period, the one of the Dohnányi Serenade in C with Heifetz and Feuermann, was reissued recently on RCA AGL1-4942.

Those familiar with Kapell's work, either through recordings or from live performances, may well call to mind the words Grillparzer wrote for the headstone of Franz Schubert, who died at about the same age: "Music has here entombed a rich treasure—but far fairer hopes." There is at present only one Kapell record in the active catalog: his famous recording of the Khachaturian Concerto, with Koussevitzky, and the equally brilliant one of Prokofiev's Third Piano Concerto, with Antal Dorati conducting the Dallas Symphony Orchestra, both issued originally on 78s, have been brought together in a very successful digitally remastered reissue in RCA's Gold Seal series (AGL1-5266). This encourages the hope that there may be reissues of some of the even finer recordings actually taped in the microgroove era—Rachmaninoff's Rhapsody on a Theme of Paganini, with Fritz Reiner conducting the Robin Hood Dell Orchestra of Philadelphia, the same composer's Second Concerto, with the same orchestra under William Steinberg, the Beethoven Second Concerto, with Steinberg and the NBC Symphony Orchestra, and, for a solo showpiece, the *Mephisto* Waltz no. 1 of Liszt.

Walter Gieseking

SIDE 8 BAND 2

Johannes Brahms (1833–1897)
Intermezzo in B minor, op. 119, no. 1
Intermezzo in A major, op. 118, no. 2

Gieseking, piano.
Recorded 22 June 1951, Zurich. Included through the courtesy of EMI Records, Ltd.

SIDE 9 BAND 1

Claude Debussy (1862–1918)
Suite bergamasque
    I. Prélude
    II. Menuet
    III. Clair de lune
    IV. Passepied

Gieseking, piano.
Recorded 22 September 1951, London. Included through the courtesy of EMI Records, Ltd.

Walter Gieseking (1895–1956), a German, was born in France and spent a good deal of his youth in that country and Italy. That may explain, in part, his exceptional response to the music of Debussy and Ravel, but another explanation might be found in Gieseking's early attention to the music of his own time, a facet of his career that tends to be forgotten now, perhaps because it was not documented on records. (The two French masters, after all, wrote much of their music during Gieseking's lifetime.)

Apart from his eminence in Debussy and Ravel, Gieseking is remembered for his authoritative way with Beethoven and Mozart, his stylish playing of Bach and Handel, and his poetic interpretations of Brahms and Grieg (the latter's *Lyric Pieces* as well as the concerto). His was the great recording of the Liszt E-flat Concerto on 78s, and in fact he played *everything*. When he came to the U.S. after World War II, people who knew him only from recordings were surprised to find him offering the Rachmaninoff Second Concerto, but it was not new territory for him: in 1936 Rachmaninoff was so impressed by Gieseking's broadcast performance of his Third Concerto that he decided to stop playing that work himself and leave it to Gieseking and Horowitz. In the early years of his career Gieseking made a point of presenting works by Busoni, Szymanowski, Schoenberg, and Hindemith in his recitals, and it was his premiere performance of the Pfitzner concerto in 1923 that really established him as a major figure. He chose the Hindemith concerto for his American debut in 1926. Gieseking never separated "modern music" from "the classics," but enjoyed performing in both categories all his life; he gave his first Beethoven sonata cycle in Hanover at the age of twenty, just five years after entering the conservatory there. Chamber music as well as solo works and concertos also attracted his attention throughout his career.

At the end of World War II Gieseking became a controversial figure for a few years. Accused of having been a Nazi collaborator, he was actually prevented from giving some of his scheduled performances in the United States. He was eventually cleared of that taint, however, and did perform here. He was only sixty-one when he died, and his last recordings show him at the height of his powers. He had made new recordings of all of Debussy's piano music and all the Mozart sonatas and had nearly completed cycles of the Beethoven sonatas and concertos. It is from these postwar recordings that those included in this collection were selected.

Clarity distinguished Gieseking's approach to everything he played. His Mozart was crisply articulated yet warmly communica-

125

tive; his Beethoven was majestic, dramatic, warmhearted, but always governed by a prime regard for musical values and an unfailing sense of proportion. There was neither inflation nor condescension in his playing of the Grieg *Lyric Pieces,* in which, as in the Schubert impromptus, he instinctively found the essential poetry of the music and the proper scale for its most effective projection. This comment applies as well to the two Brahms intermezzi presented here.

Brahms composed a total of eighteen intermezzi, distributed in various collections of piano pieces. Three are among the eight pieces in op. 76, composed in 1878; all the rest are in the final groupings, opp. 116–119, all composed in 1892. (The third of the four ballades, op. 10, of 1854, is also subtitled "Intermezzo.") The intermezzo was a form Brahms also substituted for a conventional scherzo in several of his orchestral and chamber works. The piano intermezzi are for the most part introspective, contemplative pieces. Philipp Spitta, the Bach scholar, described those of op. 118 as "pieces for leisured expression and contemplation in stillness and solitude."

Debussy composed two settings of Paul Verlaine's poem *Clair de lune* ("Moonlight")—one at about the time he turned twenty, in 1882, the other nine years later as the concluding song in the first of his *Fêtes galantes* cycles. The poem is thought to have been the inspiration for the *Suite bergamasque,* too, since Verlaine's text makes reference to *"masques et bergamasques"* and the third of the suite's four movements is also titled *Clair de lune.* (This piece on its own, of course, has become one of Debussy's best-known works, not only in its original form but perhaps even more in various orchestral arrangements.) The suite was composed in 1890, a year before the *Fêtes galantes,* and was revised and published fifteen years later. The title of the work and those of its three other movements—1. *Prélude;* 2. *Menuet;* 4. *Passepied*—bespeak Debussy's reverence for the great founders of the French keyboard tradition, Rameau and Couperin, and for the Watteau-ish impressions evoked by both their music and Verlaine's verses.

At about the time of Gieseking's death, his Debussy interpretations began to be questioned in some quarters: it was suggested that his "gossamer" approach robbed the music of its vitality, and other pianists adopted a bolder, more overtly dramatic style in playing these works. Like virtually all music of substance, Debussy's perhaps allows for more than a single convincing approach, but no other approach to it has proved to be more lastingly convincing than

Walter Gieseking   NYPL

Gieseking's. He alone seemed to capture the unique combination of delicacy and true vitality that is the essence of Debussy's own unique style in creating this music.

Not all of Gieseking's Debussy is available at present. His prewar recordings of the two books of preludes, the *Children's Corner* Suite, and the *Suite bergamasque* are in Odyssey set 32 36 0021. The postwar recording of the two books of preludes are in EMI import set RLS 752, together with the *Estampes* and *Images*. A single disc of fifteen early pieces, including the *Danse* and the two Arabesques, is still circulating and is a gem (Angel 35026). Although he recorded all of Ravel's unaccompanied works, these have disappeared except for a few pieces on Seraphim 60210.

A two-disc set of Brahms's piano music (opp. 76, 79, 116, 118, and 119) is available on the Seraphim label (IB-6117), and another contains thirty-one of Grieg's *Lyric Pieces* (IB-6114). The complete cycle of Mozart sonatas and other piano pieces fill eleven discs in three Seraphim sets (6047, 6048, 6049).

In the concerto category, two discs are outstanding. On Odyssey 32 16 0371 Gieseking and Karajan, with the Philharmonia Orches-

tra, collaborate in a superb account of Mozart's Concerto no. 23 in A
(K. 488) and a good one of Beethoven's no. 4 in G major. Although
Gieseking was active late enough to record the *Emperor* in stereo, with
Alceo Galliera, the first of his three recordings of Beethoven's last
concerto, made with Bruno Walter and the Vienna Philharmonic in
March 1938, is the one that is the most persuasive, and the sound
stands up well on Turnabout THS-65011. (That, incidentally, was
one of Walter's last recordings in Vienna until after the war and the
second of only four piano concerto recordings he made in his entire
life. The first, also with the Philharmoniker, was of the Mozart D
minor Concerto, with himself as soloist; the third was another
Emperor, with Rudolf Serkin and the New York Philharmonic, and the
last was the Schumann Piano Concerto, with Eugene Istomin and a
studio orchestra.)

Gieseking's one chamber music recording is the Seraphim disc of
the Mozart and Beethoven quintets for piano and winds, with the
Philharmonia Wind Quartet (60368).

Dennis Brain

SIDE 9 BAND 2

Wolfgang Amadeus Mozart (1756–1791)
Horn Concerto no. 3 in E-flat major, K. 447
     I. Allegro
    II. Romanze (Larghetto)
   III. Allegro

Brain, French horn; Philharmonia Orchestra, Herbert von Karajan cond.
Recorded 13 November 1953, London. Included through the courtesy of EMI Records, Ltd.

Like Dinu Lipatti and Emanuel Feuermann, Dennis Brain died in
his thirties; in his case it was not disease but an automobile accident
that brought a premature end to a brilliant career. Now, nearly thirty
years after his death, Brain (1921–1957) is still widely regarded as the
incomparable master of his instrument. His talent might be said to
have been inherited in part: his father, Aubrey Brain (1893–1955),

his paternal uncle Alfred Brain (1885–1966), and their father were all horn players; his older brother, Leonard (1915–1975), was a respected oboist. Aubrey Brain, in fact, was probably the most admired of all horn players in the years between the two world wars; he made a famous recording of the concerto his son and pupil performs in this set (with cadenzas by his wife, Dennis's mother), and when Dennis was still a teenager (he made his professional debut at seventeen) they recorded the big Mozart Divertimento, K. 334, together with the Léner Quartet.

More than his father, more than any of his colleagues or predecessors, Dennis Brain expanded the acknowledged capacities of his instrument for flexibility, subtlety, expressiveness, and color. After the war he was the obvious choice as principal horn in Beecham's new Royal Philharmonic and in the Philharmonia Orchestra that Walter Legge created for recording; Brain held both chairs until his death. He organized a wind quintet and performed and recorded chamber music frequently. Hindemith's Horn Concerto and Benjamin Britten's Serenade for Tenor, Horn, and Strings are among the several works composed for him.

Dennis Brain believed that the performer could determine the quality of tone produced by any horn, and to illustrate this he would attach his mouthpiece to a length of garden hose. In one of Gerard Hoffnung's humorous festivals Brain played and recorded a concerto by Leopold Mozart on such an instrument. He did acknowledge, however, that certain instruments had characteristics or capacities of their own, and in 1951 he switched from his French instrument to a German double horn which enabled him to produce an even bigger, more voluptuous sound than he had until then. The Mozart Concerto recorded here is performed on the German instrument.

Almost as soon as the Philharmonia Orchestra was created, after World War II, Brain recorded Mozart's Second Concerto (K. 417), with Walter Susskind conducting, and even before that he recorded the Fourth Horn Concerto with the Hallé Orchestra under an unnamed conductor. In the early years of microgroove, when Herbert von Karajan was conspicuously active with the Philharmonia, Brain recorded all four Mozart concertos with him, and also the *Sinfonia concertante* for wind quartet and orchestra. With Wolfgang Sawallisch conducting, he recorded the two Strauss concertos, and he did the Hindemith concerto with the composer conducting.

Of Mozart's four horn concertos, three are real concertos, all in

129

Dennis Brain   EMI Records (Derek Allen)

E-flat (nos. 2–4, K. 417, 447 and 495); the other is a curious bracketing of two unrelated movements in D major (no. 1, K. 412). There are also a fragment of an additional concerto in E major, listed as K. 494a, and an independent rondo in E-flat, K. 371, possibly intended as a concerto finale. Most of these works, possibly all of them, as well as the Quintet for horn and strings (K. 407) were composed for Mozart's friend Ignaz Leutgeb, who was principal horn of the Archbishop's orchestra in Salzburg until 1777, when he moved to Vienna and became a cheesemonger. Sir George Grove, the founder of the famous musical dictionary, wrote: "There must have been something attractive about Leutgeb personally, for with no one does Mozart appear to have played so many tricks." The inscriptions in the scores suggest that the two shared the same sort of raw humor. Mozart saluted Leutgeb as "ass, ox and fool" in the score of the Second Concerto, and in that of the Fourth he teased him with comments and instructions written out in inks of different colors. In all these works, though, he provided him—and all the horn players that followed—with showpieces of a very high order.

The most popular of these concertos is no. 3, composed in the mid-1780s. (The date appears to be uncertain, though we know no. 2 was written in May 1783 and no. 4 in June 1786.) The opening movement boasts one of the most attractive themes to be found in any of Mozart's wind concertos, lending itself to both sportive and caressing gestures. The second movement is a *Romanze* marked *Larghetto,* filled with both nobility and warmth of heart. The finale, like those of the companion concertos, is a "hunting" rondo with a beguilingly energetic theme; that of the *Romanze* is recalled before the end.

Dennis Brain's record of all the Mozart concertos with Karajan is still in circulation (Angel 35092). His earlier recording of the Second Concerto, with Susskind, is part of the memorial program *The Art of Dennis Brain* (Seraphim 60040), which includes also the Beethoven Horn Sonata (Denis Matthews, piano), two movements from a Mozart divertimento for winds (K. 289), Schumann's Adagio and Allegro, op. 70, and works by Dittersdorf, Haydn, and Dukas.

A few months before his death, Brain performed the Brahms Horn Trio with Max Salpeter, violin, and Cyril Preedy, piano, for the BBC; this performance has been put on a record with a somewhat earlier one of Mozart's Quintet for Horn and Strings and a somewhat later one of a Marin Marais piece called *Le Basque* (BBC 22175). Another horn trio, by Sir Lennox Berkeley, with Manoug Parikian, violin, and Colin Horsley, piano, is paired with Mozart's Piano and Wind Quintet (Horsley and the Dennis Brain Wind Ensemble) on Seraphim 60073. Brain is the hornist in another recording of the same Mozart work, this time coupled with Beethoven's similar quintet, as a member of the Philharmonia Wind Quartet with Walter Gieseking at the piano, on Seraphim 60368. The two Strauss concertos with Sawallisch are on Angel 35496.

The Hindemith Concerto is available on Angel S-35491 and as part of a three-disc import whose other contents—with one or two exceptions, including the aforementioned Leopold Mozart Concerto on the garden hose—duplicate those of the Seraphim and Angel releases (EMI RLS 7701). More duplications turn up on another memorial disc, together with demonstration portions by Brain and spoken reminiscences by his colleagues (Arabesque 8071). The earlier of Brain's two recordings of the Britten Serenade—with Peter Pears and the Boyd Neel Orchestra conducted by Britten—is another import item, English Decca Eclipse ECM-814.

131

Rudolf Serkin

Robert Schumann (1810–1856)
Piano Quintet in E-flat major, op. 44
    I. Allegro brillante
    II. In moda d'una Marcia—Un poco largamente—Allegro
    III. Scherzo—Molto vivace
    IV. Allegro ma non troppo

Serkin, piano; Busch Quartet: Adolf Busch, Gosta Andreasson, violins; Karl Doktor, viola;
Hermann Busch, cello.
Recorded 22 May 1942. Included through the courtesy of CBS Special Products.

One of the handful of musicians represented in this collection and
still actively performing, Rudolf Serkin (born in Eger, Bohemia, in
1903) represents the combination of profundity and exuberance that
characterized the Central European tradition at its brightest and
best. As soloist, chamber music player, and pedagogue, he has
enriched American musical life for nearly half a century and presided
over one of the country's more significant festival/school enterprises,
Marlboro, which itself came into being through the collective enthusiasm of the remarkable dynasty of which Serkin himself is now the
chief figure. He is a symbol of continuity in the most vital sense.

Serkin grew up in Vienna, where, among his more expected studies, he took composition lessons from Arnold Schoenberg. At the age
of twelve he performed with the Vienna Symphony Orchestra under
Oskar Nedbal; five years later, in beginning his career in earnest, he
performed with Adolf Busch's chamber orchestra in Berlin, initiating
the closest personal and professional relationships of his life. He lived
with the Busch family for a time, continued to perform with the
Busch Chamber Players and the Busch Quartet, formed a violin-and-
piano duo with Adolf Busch, and played in the Busch Trio with Adolf
and his cellist brother Hermann. In 1935 Serkin married Adolf
Busch's daughter Irene; their son Peter, born in 1947, has established
himself now as an important pianist in his own right, and another
son, John, is a horn player.

Adolf Busch (1891–1952) was the second son of a Westphalian instrument-maker who had once been a traveling musician. Adolf's older brother, Fritz (1890–1951), was one of the most respected conductors of his time, in both the opera house and the concert hall. Yehudi Menuhin, who was sent to study with Adolf Busch by his other great teacher George Enescu, has described Adolf as "the greatest exponent in his day of the pure German classical tradition." He was an outstanding pedagogue, a composer of real substance, and a first-rate violinist; he performed the Beethoven and Brahms concertos but preferred chamber music to virtuoso pieces. In Vienna in 1913, while he was concertmaster of the Konzertverein Orchestra, he founded the Wiener Konzertvereins-Quartett; after World War I he reorganized it as the Busch Quartet, which, with various changes in personnel, was to perform more or less continuously in Europe and America until Busch's death. A third brother, Hermann (1897–1975), who formed the Trio with Adolf and Serkin, was the Quartet's cellist from 1930. The Busch Quartet was especially revered for its warmhearted realizations of the Beethoven quartets and the German Romantic repertory in general. The Busch Chamber Players were organized to perform the works of Bach and Handel and those of Mozart that could be undertaken by a smallish orchestra.

It was with Adolf Busch that Serkin made his American debut in 1933, at the Library of Congress in Washington; three years later he made his historic New York Philharmonic debut with Toscanini conducting, and three years after that he came to the United States to stay, setting up residence in Philadelphia where he served on the faculty of the Curtis Institute of Music for nearly forty years, the last half of that period (until 1977) as the school's director. He formed an especially close relationship with Eugene Ormandy and the Philadelphia Orchestra, and in 1952, together with Adolf and Hermann Busch and flutists Marcel Moÿse and his son Louis (both associated with the Busch Chamber Players), he founded the Marlboro Music Festival and its school in Vermont, where Casals, the Budapest Quartet, and many other now legendary figures have been active over the last three decades. Serkin today is still director of Marlboro and continues, in his eighties, his vigorous schedule of concerts, recitals, and recordings.

Most of Serkin's early recordings, made in Europe, were with Busch or one or the other of his ensembles. His recorded surveys of the great solo works and the Brahms and Beethoven concertos began only after his arrival in America, and the emphasis on chamber music, fortunately, never diminished. In addition to recordings with the Busches, he recorded sonatas with Casals and more recently with Mstislav Rostropovich. Since Serkin's recording activity has continued into the era of digital recording and the compact disc, he has, not surprisingly, remade several of his basic repertory titles (some concertos as many as four times). His stereophonic remake of the Schumann Quintet, with the Budapest Quartet, has enjoyed a well-deserved success, but the earlier one he made on 78s with the Busch Quartet exhibits a spontaneity and homogeneity of style that is possible only among performers who have lived with each other and the music as closely as these had. For many listeners, this version of the Schumann Quintet remains the touchstone for performances of this work.

The piano quintet is a category that has been much less favored over the years than one might have thought. Neither Mozart nor Beethoven nor Haydn composed a quintet for piano and strings, and the one Schubert wrote, called *The Trout,* is not for piano and string quartet but for piano, string trio, and double bass. Brahms, Schumann, Dvořák, Franck, and Shostakovich each made one contribution to this genre; Gabriel Fauré and Ernest Bloch each left us two. It would be hard for most of us to think of many other examples; at the same time, one notes that nearly all of those just cited are among the respective composers' very finest works. None, surely, is more beloved than the earliest of them, Schumann's, which represents the summit of his achievement in the realm of chamber music.

It was Schumann's custom for some time to concentrate on a single category of music at a time. Thus in 1840 he produced mostly songs, in 1841 he focused on the production of symphonic works, and 1842 was a year for chamber music. In that year he produced all three of his string quartets (op. 41), the Piano Quartet (op. 47), and the quintet recorded here, which he dedicated to Clara. All of these works exude Schumann's characteristic expressiveness, his Romantic impetuosity mixed with episodes of melancholy bordering on the tragic. The opening of the op. 44 Quintet is as lusty as that of the *Rhenish* Symphony in the same key, still eight years in the future when this work was written; a lyrical second theme is given to the cello (the string instrument surely closest to Schumann's heart) and then to the viola, and another motif is introduced by the first violin. The second movement is headed *In modo d'una Marcia* and is apparently a funeral

134

Rudolf Serkin   NYPL

march, with a sad but flowing melody in the middle section and a
demonic *agitato* episode near the end. A sharp contrast is provided by
the ensuing *Scherzo,* which, like so many of Schumann's scherzos, has
two trios of strikingly different character. The final movement finds
vigorous rhythms and melodic ideas tumbling out after one another
in dizzying spontaneity, with a fine summing-up provided in the form
of a reprise of the work's opening in the coda.

While his early studies with Schoenberg had little effect, apparently, in directing his interest to the music of his own time, Serkin has
performed contemporary material, and as recently as the 1960s he
recorded concertos by Bartók and Prokofiev. It is with the music of
Bach, Beethoven, Mozart, Schubert, and Brahms that he remains
most strongly identified, though, and in his eighties he is working his
way through a new recorded cycle of the Mozart concertos with
Claudio Abbado and the London Symphony Orchestra for Deutsche
Grammophon. Of the dozens of his recordings in the current catalogue, these are especially recommended, both as particularly representative of Serkin's style and simply as outstanding statements of the
respective works:

135

Beethoven: Piano Concerto no. 1 in C major, op. 15, w/Philadelphia Orch. u/d Eugene Ormandy; Sonata no. 26 in E-flat, op 81a (*Les Adieux*). CBS MY-37807.

Beethoven: Piano Concerto no. 2 in B-flat, op. 19; Mozart: Concerto no. 27 in B-flat, K. 595, w/Philadelphia Orch. u/d Ormandy. CBS MS-6839.

Beethoven: Piano Concerto no. 4 in G major, op. 58, w/Boston Symphony Orch. u/d Seiji Ozawa. Telarc DG-10064.

Beethoven: Piano Concerto no. 5 in E-flat, op. 73 (*Emperor*), w/ Boston Symphony Orch. u/d Ozawa. Telarc DG-10065.

Beethoven: Concerto in C for Violin, Cello, and Piano, op. 56; Sonata no. 24 in F-sharp, op. 78; Fantasie in G minor, op. 77. CBS MP-38895.

Beethoven: Sonata no. 29 in B-flat, op. 106 (*Hammerklavier*); Bagatelles, op. 119. CBS MP-38893.

Beethoven: 33 Variations on a Waltz by A. Diabelli, op. 120. CBS MP-38780 or CSP AML-5246.

Brahms: Concerto no. 1 in D minor, op. 15, w/Cleveland Orch. u/d George Szell. CBS MY-37803.

Brahms: Concerto no. 2 in B-flat, op. 83, w/Cleveland Orch. u/d Szell. CBS MY-37258.

Brahms: Piano Quintet in F minor, op. 34, w/Busch Quartet. Turnabout THS-65061.

Brahms: Cello Sonatas, opp. 38 & 99, w/Mstislav Rostropovich. Deutsche Grammophon 2532.073.

Brahms: Variations and Fugue on a Theme by Handel, op. 24; Intermezzi and Rhapsody, op. 119. CBS M-35177.

Mendelssohn: Piano Concertos nos. 1 & 2; Capriccio brillant, op. 22. Schumann: Piano Concerto in A minor, op. 54; Introduction and Allegro in D minor, op. 134, w/Philadelphia Orch. u/d Ormandy. CBS MG-32042.

Mozart: Piano Concertos no. 14 in E-flat, K. 449, & no. 17 in G major, K. 453, w/Columbia Symphony u/d Alexander Schneider. CBS MP-38771.

Mozart: Piano Concertos no. 19 in F, K. 459, & no. 20 in D minor, K. 466, w/Columbia Symphony u/d Szell. CBS MY-37236.

Schubert: Quintet in A major, op. 114/D. 667 (*The Trout*), w/ Marlboro group. CBS MY-37234.

In addition to the Brahms Quintet with Serkin, cited above, the Busch Quartet's recording of Schubert's Quartet no. 14 in D minor (*Death and the Maiden*) has been reissued on a domestic LP (Turnabout TV 34828). The Busch prewar recordings of several Beethoven quartets have been reissued in Germany and Japan and occasionally turn up in the import lists.

Nathan Milstein and Vladimir Horowitz

SIDE 11 BAND 1

Johannes Brahms (1833–1897)
Violin Sonata no. 3 in D minor, op. 108
    I. Allegro
    II. Adagio
    III. Un poco presto e con sentimento
    IV. Presto agitato

Milstein, violin; Horowitz, piano.
Recorded 22–29 June 1950, New York. Included through the courtesy of RCA Records.

Vladimir Horowitz and Nathan Milstein, both born in Russia in 1904, are, like their contemporary Rudolf Serkin, still commanding respect for the virtuosity they exhibit today rather than mere sentimental acknowledgement of past stature. Milstein and Horowitz began their careers together. Within months of the Paris premiere of Prokofiev's First Violin Concerto and before that work was heard in the Soviet Union in orchestral form, they performed it in Moscow as a violin and piano piece in 1924; in the following year they left for the West, never to return. They came to the United States at the end of that decade, together with the cellist Gregor Piatigorsky, with whom they performed trios in New York in 1930. (They never recorded as a trio, but Milstein made a single recording with Piatigorsky—the Brahms Double Concerto, Reiner conducting—and one with Horowitz.)

Horowitz may be regarded as one of the last, and perhaps the most remarkable ever, of the legendary keyboard giants whose staggering technique enabled them to make everything they touched their own—who not only informed the music with their own personalities but in many cases altered it to suit their styles. In terms of technical brilliance, Horowitz is the most astounding of all pianists, his name evoking the adjective "superhuman." While he has brought down many a house with the sort of miniatures and transcriptions that were the bread-and-butter of the nineteenth-century barnstormers, he is at the same time capable of reaching exalted heights in great works—an artist of profound depth, rare insight, and an unfailing sense of style which enabled him to fill even the showpieces with elegance. Another adjective triggered by his name is "aristocratic."

Milstein represents a somewhat different sort of musical aristocracy. He has been identified throughout his career with the German and Viennese classics, and has his own definition of the term "virtuosity," which to him means not showmanship but "the highest degree of professional excellence." He likes to distinguish, too, between technique and mere dexterity: "Technique is not just a matter of muscular control; it means adjusting the medium to what I want to do." His naturally sweet tone has never been allowed to be, or even to seem to be, an end in itself. Boris Schwarz described him as "perhaps the least Russian of all the great Russian violinists . . . he is not throbbing, he is not emotional in the accepted sense of the word. His violinistic instincts are controlled by musical intellect. . . . His playing is a rare combination of classical taste and technical perfection. Yet he can be a dazzling technician when he tosses off his own *Paganiniana* or his new transcription of Liszt's *Mephisto* Waltz. The effortless nonchalance with which he achieves sophisticated technical feats is amazing. Milstein's greatest admirers are his fellow violinists, who understand the underlying intricacy of his flawless mechanism—and that included Kreisler, who considered himself an old friend and admirer. That Milstein did not achieve the world renown of Heifetz is a strange quirk of fate; certainly Heifetz is the only one to whom he can be compared."

Both Horowitz and Milstein had some renowned teachers, but their extraordinary native gifts were of greater consequence. Milstein has remarked that what one hears "about the great teachers amounts to no more than myths. Stolyarsky used to eat an egg when we played for him in Odessa, and Auer was really no teacher at all—he picked only students who didn't need him." From the age of thirteen Milstein had no teacher, though he had some coaching from Ysaÿe in

Nathan Milstein   NYPL   *Vladimir Horowitz   NYPL*

1926. He made his debut in Russia at the age of ten, and eight years later he had the experience of performing in the Glazunov Concerto with the composer conducting. He chose that work for his American debut, with Stokowski and the Philadelphia Orchestra in 1929, a year after Horowitz made his U.S. debut in the Tchaikovsky First Concerto with Beecham in New York.

The late Samuel Barber's Piano Sonata was composed for Horowitz, who made the first recording of it, but he has not introduced many other contemporary works. Nor is he the pianist one looks to for a complete Beethoven sonata cycle: he has always chosen what appeals to him from the works of Beethoven, Mozart, Schubert, Schumann, Clementi, Liszt, Chopin, Scriabin—and he is extremely selective about adding to his repertoire. He is one of the very few pianists of first rank who have not recorded all the big concertos; he has in fact recorded only four concertos (though one of these twice and another three times). His first appearance with an orchestra in some three decades was with the New York Philharmonic in 1978, to mark the fiftieth anniversary of his American debut with that orchestra. The Rachmaninoff Third Concerto, recorded live on that occasion (Eugene Ormandy conducting), is a work long considered his personal property by many—among them Rachmaninoff himself, who was so delighted with Horowitz's playing of the work that he made some alterations in the score to make it a more effective vehicle

139

for him. The first of Horowitz's three recordings of it was made years before Rachmaninoff recorded it himself. His next concerto recordings—of the Tchaikovsky First and Brahms Second concertos—were made in 1940 with his father-in-law Arturo Toscanini; in the early 1950s he remade the Rachmaninoff with Fritz Reiner, with whom he also recorded Beethoven's *Emperor* Concerto.

Part of the mystique surrounding Horowitz probably has to do with the rarity of his appearances. For a dozen years (1953–65) he withdrew from concert and recital activity altogether, though he made some recordings in that period. When he returned to the recital stage in 1965, eager fans spent the night outside Carnegie Hall waiting for tickets to go on sale (and his wife sent coffee to the ticket line). Since then he has toured fairly regularly but on a relaxed schedule, with all performances—even at the White House—given on Sunday afternoons at four. Milstein, on the other hand, has continued without interruption to perform the works he loves, both in solo recitals and with orchestras in Europe and America. He has given regular master classes in Switzerland as well.

The only recording Milstein and Horowitz made together (or, in any event, the only one issued commercially) is this one of the last of Brahms's three sonatas for violin and piano—an apt choice in this context since it happens to be one of the few such works (and the only one by Brahms) in which the two instruments begin together. The sonata was composed between 1886 and 1888 and was dedicated to the great pianist and conductor Hans von Bülow, who had become a champion of Brahms's music. Bülow's life and personality are said to have inspired Brahms to write the sort of music this work turned out to be, markedly different from its two predecessors.

Each of Brahms's two earlier violin sonatas is in three movements and has a ruminative character. The D minor is in four movements, more overtly dramatic and tightly organized. Even in the reflective passages of the first movement one is aware of a certain restlessness and propulsiveness, and the heartfelt *Adagio* which follows is also marked by a sense of conciseness and forward thrust. The tiny scherzo, marked *Un poco presto e con sentimento,* has no trio, but combines a motoric rhythm with an essentially pathetic theme. The concluding movement is a vigorous *Presto agitato* whose second theme alludes to one in the corresponding position in the Piano Quintet in F minor Brahms composed more than twenty years earlier.

Virtually all of Horowitz's recordings are in circulation now, on dozens of records. RCA has been reissuing its early ones in new packagings, and recording all his recitals live during the last dozen years or so. All four of his concertos—the Tchaikovsky and Brahms with Toscanini, the Rachmaninoff and Beethoven with Reiner—have been collected in a four-disc set (RCA CRM4-0914). The premiere recording of the Rachmaninoff (no. 3 in D, op. 30), made in London with Albert Coates conducting, comes with Haydn's final sonata as a little bonus on Seraphim 60063; the 1978 live stereo version with Ormandy is on RCA CRL1-2633.

Of the records taken from recent recitals, one of the most appealing is ARL1-4322, which contains 1979/80 performances of Clementi's big *Sonata quasi concerto* in C major, Chopin's *Barcarolle* and two of his etudes, and three pieces by Rachmaninoff: the Prelude in G minor, *Moment musical* in E-flat minor, and the *Polka V.R.*

An RCA collection labeled *Concert Encores* (RCA ARM1-2717), recorded between 1942 and 1951, displays Horowitz's stunning technical wizardry and, in some of the pieces, his no less remarkable gift for poetry and delicacy. Included are his own *Carmen* Variations, his transcriptions of Mussorgsky's song "By the Water" and Sousa's "Stars and Stripes Forever," his arrangements of the Liszt settings of Mendelssohn's *A Midsummer Night's Dream* Wedding March and Saint-Saëns's *Danse macabre,* the Bach/Busoni *Nun komm', der Heiden Heiland,* three of Mendelssohn's *Songs without Words,* the *Rondo alla turca* from Mozart's Sonata in A major, K. 331, Prokofiev's Toccata, "The Doll's Serenade" from Debussy's *Children's Corner,* and two pieces by Moszkowski: the Etude in A-flat, op. 72, no. 1, and the dazzling *Etincelles.*

The Barber Sonata and Prokofiev's Seventh Sonata are on RCA ARM1-2952, with two Scriabin preludes and two etudes. Schumann's *Kinderszenen* and Toccata are on CBS MS-6411, with three Scarlatti sonatas, a Schubert impromptu, and more Scriabin. Two full discs of major Scriabin works—CBS M-31620 and the deleted RCA LM-2005—are especially valuable. Of his several Liszt recordings, the Sonata in B minor and *Funérailles* show him at his best (Seraphim 60114).

The Brahms sonata presented here is not Horowitz's only recording of chamber music. He was heard in the CBS Carnegie Hall commemorative set (M2X-34256) in a movement of Tchaikovsky's trio with Isaac Stern and Mstislav Rostropovich, in the Rachmaninoff Cello Sonata with Rostropovich, and as accompanist (!) to Dietrich

Fischer-Dieskau in Schumann's *Dichterliebe*.

Milstein's current discography is much smaller than Horowitz's, but it contains several gems in fine, up-to-date sound. His second recording of the Bach partitas and sonatas for unaccompanied violin (Deutsche Grammophon 2709.047) is in the nature of a monumental testament. His record of the two Bach solo concertos and two by Vivaldi, conducted by himself (Angel RL-32073), is a model of style, sensitivity, and illuminating intelligence. The remake of the Brahms concerto with Eugen Jochum and the Vienna Philharmonic (DG 2530.592) is one of the finest accounts of that work, and the pairing of the Tchaikovsky and Mendelssohn concertos, with the same orchestra under Claudio Abbado (DG 2530.359), is in the same class.

The Glazunov concerto, which figured so prominently in Milstein's early career, is coupled with the Dvořák concerto on Angel RL-32034, with Rafael Frühbeck de Burgos conducting the New Philharmonia in both. The once popular concerto of Karl Goldmark receives an extremely sympathetic performance on Seraphim S-60238, with the two Beethoven romances on side 2; Harry Blech conducts the Goldmark, Milstein himself the Beethoven. Milstein's own brilliant *Paganiniana*, a set of unaccompanied variations, is on Deutsche Grammophon Signature 410.843-1, with Georges Pludermacher, piano, joining the violinist in Schubert's *Rondeau Brillant,* a Stravinsky piece, a Geminiani sonata, and Milstein's arrangements of pieces by Mussorgksy, Liszt, and Kodály.

Reginald Kell

SIDE 11 BAND 2

Carl Maria von Weber (1786–1826)
Clarinet Concertino in E-flat major, op. 26
  I. Adagio ma non troppo
  II. Tema con variazioni—Andante
  III. Allegro

Kell, clarinet; unidentified orchestra, Walter Goehr cond.
Recorded 4 July 1939, London. Included through the courtesy of EMI Records, Ltd.

Reginald Kell (1906–1981) was the first internationally recognized clarinet virtuoso of modern times. Although this great English musician was not the pioneer Casals was in terms of revising the character of his instrument or its actual sound, he did much to bring about a new style of playing and a new appreciation on the part of a large public.

The clarinet, an eighteenth-century addition to the wind family, is an instrument whose capacities for voluptuous coloring and warm expressiveness made it especially welcome at the beginning of the Romantic era—and indeed made a conspicuous contribution to the character of instrumental music in that era. Both Schubert and his senior contemporary Weber used the clarinet prominently in their orchestral and chamber music. Mozart's earlier and Brahms's later works for the instrument and the virtuosi who inspired them, have been discussed previously in the Primrose/Kapell section. Weber's inspiration was the Bavarian clarinetist Heinrich Bärmann, for whom he composed a quintet, several pieces for clarinet and piano, and three concerted works.

With this sort of background, Kell did not have to establish his instrument himself. There were in fact other noted clarinetists in the generation before his, most notably Simeon Bellison in New York and the Frenchman Louis Cahuzac, who was active as a performer into his seventies. It was Kell, though—at about the same time Benny Goodman was giving occasional performances of classical music as a supplement to his jazz activity—who became a full-fledged celebrity,

Reginald Kell   *EMI Records (Sasha)*

paving the way, as it were, for today's Gervase de Peyer and the younger Richard Stoltzman. Kell acknowledged the influence of oboist Léon Goossens in developing his particular style, which involved a subtle and imaginative use of vibrato for expressive effect. Sir Thomas Beecham picked Kell as his principal clarinetist when he founded the London Philharmonic Orchestra in 1932, and after World War II Kell played in the newly formed Philharmonia Orchestra until 1948, when he moved to the United States to take up a career as soloist. He performed with many of our leading orchestras and chamber music groups and made several recordings here. His recording career began much earlier, though, during his pre-war service in the London Philharmonic, when he made this recording of the Weber Concertino, among other works.

(The conductor in this recording, Walter Goehr, came to England from Germany in 1933 and died there in 1960 at fifty-seven. He became especially well-known through recordings, particularly in concertos with such soloists as Myra Hess and Wanda Landowska;

144

with Kell he made one of the first recordings of the Mozart Clarinet Concerto. He was the father of the composer Alexander Goehr.)

In addition to the composers cited above, Hummel, Spohr, and Beethoven also wrote for the clarinet in their chamber music at the end of the eighteenth century and early in the nineteenth; but no composer identified himself with the instrument more eloquently than Weber. Much of the dramatic coloring of *Der Freischütz* is related to or determined by the clarinet—as it is also in *Oberon* and *Euryanthe,* in the two symphonies and the surviving overtures to the forgotten stage works. Heinrich Bärmann was the solo clarinetist of the Munich Court Orchestra; Weber, who used to see him daily when he lived in Munich, referred to him as "a truly great artist and glorious man," and from the music Weber composed for him we can infer a broad good nature and a capacity for high spirits in addition to his celebrated musicianship. The concertino, comprising a slow introduction *(Andante),* a brief set of variations, and a concluding *Allegro,* was composed in about ten days and was first performed by Bärmann on 5 April 1811. The Bavarian king, Max Joseph, so enjoyed the work that he commissioned Weber to compose two full-length concertos for Bärmann; these were produced in the same year, and Bärmann played all three works with great success on his frequent tours.

Kell returned to England in 1971 and died ten years later in Frankfort, Kentucky. Although he recorded all the great clarinet works in the chamber music literature (some of them as many as four times) and many of the great concertos, the only one of his recordings that appears to be available at present outside this Smithsonian set is his Brahms Clarinet Quintet with the Busch Quartet (Japanese EMI GR 2240).

Fritz Kreisler

SIDE 12 BAND 1

Felix Mendelssohn-Bartholdy (1809–1847)
Violin Concerto in E minor, op. 64
    I. Allegro molto appassionato
    II. Andante
    III. Allegretto non troppo—Allegro molto vivace

Kreisler, violin; Berlin State Opera Orchestra, Leo Blech cond.
Recorded 9 October 1926, Berlin. Included through the courtesy of EMI Records, Ltd.

SIDE 12 BAND 2

Fritz Kreisler (1875–1962)
Liebesleid

Kreisler, violin; Carl Lamson, piano.
Recorded 14 April 1926, Camden NJ. Included through the courtesy of RCA Records.

The Viennese-born Fritz Kreisler (1875–1962) was a musician so vastly beloved—for the warmth of his personality and the charm of his compositions—that his greatness as a performer tends to be less than fully acknowledged in the blur of sentimental recollections. He was, in fact, a superb violinist, commanding an impeccable technique, a tone as pure as it was rich and expressive, and a remarkable communicativeness built on equal measures of charm and elegance. Kreisler was, all his life, first and foremost a violinist, beginning as a child prodigy and completing his formal training at the age of twelve. (In those early years he had lessons in theory from Anton Bruckner as well as violin instruction from Joseph Hellmesberger at the Vienna Conservatory, and then two years at the Paris Conservatory with Joseph Lambert Massart, the teacher of Wieniawski.) In his late teens Kreisler went through a crisis of indecision; he went back to school, took a pre-medical course (thinking to follow his father's profession), and then fulfilled his Austrian military service before finally making the commitment to a musical life. His international career was launched in earnest with an appearance as soloist with the Berlin Philharmonic under the direction of Arthur Nikisch.

Kreisler saw action in the Austrian army in World War I and received a medical discharge after being wounded. He and his American wife lived in Berlin until the Nazis came to power, then in Paris until the outbreak of World War II, when they settled in the U.S.; Kreisler became a citizen in 1943. In 1941 he was involved in a traffic accident that affected both his vision and his hearing; he last appeared in public in 1947, continued to perform light works in broadcasts until 1950, and then sold all but one of his instruments.

As the pre-eminent senior violinist of his time, Kreisler was the obvious choice, in the early 1930s, to make the first "integral" recording of the Beethoven violin sonatas (with pianist Franz Rupp, who is still active today), as he had been at the beginning of the electrical recording era to record the violin concertos of Beethoven, Brahms, and Mendelssohn. (His cadenzas for the Beethoven, in particular, and the Brahms have been taken up by many other violinists.) He began his recording activity many years earlier, in the days of thick, single-sided acoustically recorded discs, and he was perhaps the only instrumentalist in those days to enjoy a popularity comparable with Caruso's. Kreisler subsequently re-recorded the three concertos and added others by Mozart and Paganini to his discography, while throughout his long career he made innumerable recordings of his own miniatures and transcriptions. As for recordings with colleagues, he recorded a few transcriptions with his brother Hugo, a cellist, accompanied the tenor John McCormack in some song recordings, and made an early recording of the Bach Two-Violin Concerto with Efrem Zimbalist, but he recorded little chamber music aside from the Beethoven cycle with Rupp. One interesting but forgotten item in that category was a recording of his own String Quartet in A minor, played by the Kreisler Quartet, in which Hugo was cellist. Both that and the Beethoven cycle were preceded by three sonata recordings made with Rachmaninoff in 1928—works of Beethoven, Schubert, and Grieg.

In the late 1920s, when Kreisler made his first recordings of the great German concertos noted above, he was in his early fifties and at the peak of his technical and interpretive powers, and the Berlin State Opera Orchestra, with which he performed these works, was one of the finest of all recording ensembles, as confirmed in numerous recordings under such conductors as Richard Strauss, Otto Klemperer, Erich Kleiber, and Bruno Walter. The conductor for Kreisler's Berlin concerto recordings was Leo Blech (1871–1958), chief conduc-

Fritz Kreisler   EMI Records

tor of the Berlin State Opera from 1926 until the Nazis forced him out of his position ten years later. He returned to Berlin in 1949 as conductor of the Stadtische Oper. While Blech was best known in the field of opera (he composed several successful works for the stage), he was highly regarded as a symphonic conductor, and his recorded collaborations with Kreisler became classics, none of them quite matched in terms of performance by Kreisler's mid-1930s remakes with the London Philharmonic under John Barbirolli and, in the case of the Mendelssohn, Sir Landon Ronald.

Two violinists, one of them still active when Kreisler began his own career (and whom Kreisler in fact knew), were involved in the creation of Mendelssohn's Concerto. It was written for Mendelssohn's friend Ferdinand David (1810–1871), whom he brought to Leipzig in 1836 as concertmaster of the Gewandhaus Orchestra. In July 1838 Mendelssohn wrote to advise David that he was composing a concerto for him and hoped to have it ready for him to play the following year; but the premiere did not take place until 13 March 1845, for Mendelssohn didn't get to work in earnest on this composition until the summer of 1844 and completed the score only on 16 September of that year. The impetus for this delayed but marvelously productive effort probably came from the young violinist Joseph Joachim.

The Hungarian-born Joachim (1831–1907) was enormously respected, not only as a violinist and leader of a famous string quartet, but also as a composer, conductor, and pedagogue. His name is most closely linked with that of Brahms, whom he met when both were in their early twenties and whose music he championed all his life; Brahms composed both his Violin Concerto and his Double Concerto (violin, cello, and orchestra) for Joachim, and Dvořák and others composed concertos for him as well. In the spring of 1843, Joachim, not quite twelve years old, became one of the first students at Mendelssohn's new conservatory in Leipzig, where he studied composition with David and performed frequently with Mendelssohn himself as both sonata partner and concerto soloist. Mendelssohn took the lad to London in the spring of 1844 to make his debut there in the British premiere of the Beethoven Concerto—an event generally credited with having finally established that work in the repertory. It seems likely that, although Mendelssohn had promised his own concerto to David, to whom he did in fact dedicate the score, he was reminded by the young Joachim of his own achievements in his early teens and was stimulated to get to work at last on the violin concerto he had put off for so long. Joachim never claimed any part in the creation of this concerto but all his life held it in the very highest regard.

This concerto was not conceived in the epic proportions of the Brahms or Beethoven; here sentiment and the element of display are exquisitely balanced within an exceptionally well organized frame in which the near-perfection of the Italian Symphony and the *Midsummer Night's Dream* Overture are not only recalled but possibly surpassed. The framework itself was unusual for its time: where Beethoven had innovatively provided a direct link between the last two movements of his Violin Concerto (as he did in numerous other works), Mendelssohn went a step farther and joined the first two movements as well; he also eliminated the opening tutti altogether, allowing the soloist to begin the work with an unreservedly impassioned statement of the theme.

There is no common thematic material in these three interconnected movements (as there is in so many similarly constructed works); each is given its own fully developed character, Mendelssohn managing not only to charm the ear with his straightforward and elegant lyricism but also to remind us of his regard for form even while adapting it to suit his own needs.

The music Kreisler composed reflects his warm personality and, apart from his one string quartet, is mostly in the lighter vein. His operetta *Apple Blossoms* is remembered for the song "Stars in My Eyes," and the dozens of miniatures he wrote for his own instrument are cherished by violinists everywhere. In addition to the Viennese bonbons he published under his own name, Kreisler produced many other pieces which he introduced as compositions by various seventeenth- and eighteenth-century composers. The hoax was uncovered in 1935 when he admitted to the music critic Olin Downes that all those "transcriptions" were really original works "in the style of" the respective composers; he just didn't want his name appearing so many times in his program listings, he said. We would expect such a man to have a healthy sense of humor, and Kreisler demonstrated that in an encounter with a pretentious New York society matron in the 1920s. In offering him $3,000—an enormous sum in those days— to play at her home, she told him: "Of course, you are not to mingle with my guests." "I'm not to mingle with your guests?" he asked, as if he couldn't believe his ears. "Certainly *not!*" "Well, in that case, dear madam, I'll play for $2,000." *Liebesleid,* recorded with his long-time accompanist Carl Lamson, shows the tenderness and overall *Gemütlichkeit* that complemented Kreisler's elegance and humor.

While dozens of famous violinists have recorded Kreisler's miniatures in homage to the man and his musicianship, nearly all of Kreisler's own recordings have disappeared; all that remain in general circulation in the United States are to be found on one LP disc and one unrelated cassette, both from the same period of Berlin recordings as the Mendelssohn Concerto preserved here. On Angel 37925, with Franz Rupp and Michael Raucheisen alternating at the piano, Kreisler may be heard in miniatures of his own and pieces by Bach, Tchaikovsky, Dvořák, Rimsky-Korsakov, Poldini, Falla, Weber, and Cyril Scott. The Beethoven and Brahms concertos with Blech conducting have been transferred, with remarkable success, to a single cassette in In Sync's *Conductart* series, no. C4135. Finally, on a Pearl LP from England are the same recording of the Mendelssohn Concerto and Kreisler's only one of the Bruch Concerto no. 1 in G minor; the Bruch, with the London Symphony Orchestra under Eugene Goossens, was recorded acoustically in December 1924 and January 1925 and was never released in any form until it appeared on this disc (Pearl GEMM 276).

Sergei Rachmaninoff

SIDE 13

Robert Schumann (1810–1856)
Carnaval, op. 9
    1. Préambule   2. Pierrot   3. Arlequin   4. Valse
    noble   5. Eusebius   6. Florestan   7. Coquette
    8. Réplique   9. Papillons   10. ASCH-SCHA (Lettres-
    dansantes)   11. Chiarina   12. Chopin   13. Estrella
    14. Reconnaissance   15. Pantalon et Colombine   16. Valse
    allemande and Paganini intermezzo   17. Aveu   18. Prome-
    nade 19. Pause   20. Marche des Davidsbündler contre les
    Philistins

Rachmaninoff, piano.
Recorded 9, 10, 12 April 1929, Camden NJ. Included through the courtesy of RCA Records.

People who heard Sergei Rachmaninoff (1873–1943) perform do
not hesitate to pronounce him the greatest of all pianists. His huge
hands and incredible reserves of power were put at the service of a
still more incredible creativity in bringing music to life. The colors he
was able to draw from a piano have never been surpassed; the delicacy of his shadings, the intensity of his poetic vision, and the overall
vividness of his playing lent an exciting sense of spontaneity to interpretations that were in fact developed from the most serious study
and refined with the patience of a master technician. It was only in
the last thirty years of his life that Rachmaninoff came to be regarded
primarily as a pianist. Earlier he had been recognized as an important composer who was also a gifted conductor and pianist. After a
temporary setback caused by the failure of his First Symphony in
1897, he recovered his self-confidence with the aid of a psychothera-
pist and composed his immensely successful Second Concerto before
he was thirty. His similarly popular Second Symphony followed soon
after (both works won Glinka Prizes). At about that time (1906)
Rachmaninoff resigned his post as conductor at the Bolshoi Opera in
Moscow in order to live in Dresden for a time and devote himself
entirely to composing. When he came to America a few years later he

was twice offered the conductorship of the Boston Symphony Orchestra. He began to focus on a career as pianist only when he left his homeland for good after the 1917 Revolution and, having abandoned his estates, had to earn his way in the West. By the time the centenary of his birth came round in 1973, Rachmaninoff's reputation as a composer had not only been re-established but was more solid than ever. All of his symphonies and concertos are standard concert fare now, several of his heretofore unknown orchestral works have been resurrected and recorded, and it is not uncommon to encounter all-Rachmaninoff programs in the concerts of American and European orchestras.

His reputation as pianist remains undimmed, for the most enthusiastic terms used in describing his playing were never exaggerations, and he left many recordings to verify his stature—though, incredibly, not one is in general circulation now (the fifteen-LP "complete Rachmaninoff" issued by RCA on the occasion of his 1973 centenary having been quietly retired after a brief period of availability). Near the end of his life Rachmaninoff agreed to record his Third Concerto—a work he had decided to leave to Horowitz and Gieseking to perform—and his First, in order to get his new Third Symphony recorded (the last of his few recordings as conductor, all with the Philadelphia Orchestra). While he was understandably proud to be the first important composer to make "definitive" recordings of so many of his own works, it is regrettable that such a pianist recorded so little in the way of major works of other composers (his performance of the Beethoven C major Concerto was, by all accounts, one that especially ought to have been given permanence). Those he did record, by himself and with Fritz Kreisler (sonatas by Beethoven, Schubert, and Grieg), are very much worth seeking out. Rachmaninoff recorded only two large-scale works for piano alone—the Chopin Sonata no. 2 in B-flat minor and Schumann's *Carnaval;* both have enjoyed "legendary" status for more than half a century, and the latter in particular has been a prime collector's item.

Schumann gave this well-loved set of idealized dances and fantasy pieces the title *Carnaval* because he happened to finish the score at Carnival time in 1835. He appended the subtitle *Scènes mignonnes sur quatre notes;* the four notes are A, E-flat, C, and B, which in German usage are rendered as A, S, C, and H, spelling out the name of the Bohemian birthplace of Ernestine von Fricken, a young woman in whom Schumann was romantically interested at the time. As noted in

Sergei Rachmaninoff   NYPL

the tenth of these pieces, these *"Lettres dansantes"* can be rearranged to represent Schumann's own name (they are the only letters in his surname which correspond to musical notes). It must be noted further that Schumann was, despite his interest in Ernestine, already in love with Clara Wieck, who was to become his wife in 1840. A portrait of Clara appears in *Carnaval* (no. 11, Chiarina), and one of her own compositions is echoed in both that portrait and no. 3, Arlequin, while no. 13, labeled Estrella, is a portrait of Ernestine.

Aside from these romantic gestures, a broader Romantic symbolism is indicated in Schumann's description of the work as a "humoristic masked romance" in which *commedia dell' arte* characters alternate with Clara, Ernestine, and such celebrated contemporary figures as Chopin and Paganini in the spotlight, and "the outlines of adventure begin to show themselves." The whole is neatly framed by the clear relationship between the opening *Préambule* and the concluding March of the *Davidsbündler* against the Philistines. (*Davidsbündler*—the "Legion of David"—was the name adopted by the group of young idealists under Schumann's leadership, further celebrated in the *Davidsbündlertänze,* op. 6, which he composed in 1837.)

Carnaval was dedicated to neither of the ladies pictured therein, but to the Polish violinist-composer Carl Lipinski, who studied with Paganini, performed with Liszt, and subsequently received dedications from Wieniawski and other admiring colleagues. Not surprisingly, this music has been orchestrated as a ballet by more than a few composers since Schumann's time.

As already noted, all of Rachmaninoff's recordings have been withdrawn from regular commercial circulation in the United States. It is hoped that some will find their way back into the catalogue—in particular those of the Rhapsody on a Theme by Paganini, which was recorded directly after that work's world premiere with Leopold Stokowski and the Philadelphia Orchestra, and the four concertos, with the same orchestra under Stokowski and Eugene Ormandy. (All of these were most recently available on German RCA 26 35002.)

Jascha Heifetz

SIDE 14

Jean Sibelius (1865–1957)
Violin Concerto in D minor, op. 47
  I. Allegro moderato
  II. Adagio di molto
  III. Allegro ma non tanto

*Heifetz, violin; London Philharmonic Orchestra, Sir Thomas Beecham cond.
Recorded 26 November 1935, London. Included through the courtesy of EMI Records, Ltd.*

From the beginning of his career, Jascha Heifetz's name has been a synonym for the peak of musicianship in the form of violin playing— a nonpareil, a unique genius in every aspect of interpretive and technical excellence, the paragon of uncompromising integrity and taste, a lone Olympian figure. The eminent violinist and pedagogue Carl Flesch wrote in his *Memoirs:* "There has probably never been a violinist who has approached the summit of perfection more closely than

Heifetz." Some four decades later Itzhak Perlman, protégé of Isaac Stern and himself perhaps the outstanding representative of today's young generation of exceptional violinists, saluted Heifetz as simply "the greatest violinist that ever lived," and few would challenge that evaluation.

Heifetz was born in Vilna on 2 February 1901 (the twenty-sixth birthday of Fritz Kreisler). His father was a violinist; he recognized the boy's exceptional gifts and started his training early and methodically. Jascha made his public debut in Kovno at the age of seven, playing the Mendelssohn Concerto. Two years later the family moved to St. Petersburg (now Leningrad), where he became a pupil of the legendary pedagogue Leopold Auer. Only a year after Heifetz's arrival, Auer confidently sent him off to Berlin to perform a solo recital as substitute for the indisposed Pablo Casals. Five years later, on 27 October 1917, the sixteen-year-old Heifetz made his American debut at Carnegie Hall (accompanied by André Benoist). Every musician of importance who could be in New York on that day was present, and this frequently told story sums up the effect Heifetz had on his colleagues then and in the five decades to follow: Mischa Elman, Auer's last star pupil from the preceding generation, turned during the intermission to the pianist Leopold Godowsky and remarked, perspiring, "It's awfully warm in here, don't you think?" "Not for pianists," said Godowsky.

If Heifetz has indeed made it hot for violinists, he has by his extraordinary example impelled three generations of them to seek and attain higher and higher standards. In a more direct sense, nearly 200 young violinists have benefitted from his sense of responsibility in passing the torch. Auer told him, he said, "that some day I would be good enough to teach," and in the late 1950s he began giving master classes at the University of California at Los Angeles; in 1962 that famous series was transferred to the University of Southern California, and Heifetz broadened it to involve some of his distinguished chamber music associates.

When he turned forty Heifetz began recording chamber music with Feuermann, Primrose, and Rubinstein. Feuermann, who died in 1942, was replaced by Gregor Piatigorsky when the chamber music recordings resumed in 1950, and the trio (with Rubinstein) gave a few live performances at that time. The amiable relationship between the violinist and the cellist led to the establishment of the Heifetz-Piatigorsky Concerts in 1960, a series documented by many

recordings of works ranging from duos to concertos. Heifetz's last
public performance, a benefit recital given in Los Angeles in 1972 for
the Music School at USC, was the source of his last recordings. Since
then he has continued to teach and has made television films of some
of his master classes, but he makes no public appearances except
those connected with the school. (When the magazine *Stereo Review*
made him its "Musician of the Year" in 1976, on the occasion of his
seventy-fifth birthday, he declined to show up at the ceremony and
forbade anyone to accept the award on his behalf.)

Heifetz made his first recordings less than two weeks after his
American debut in 1917, and in the sixty-five years that followed he
recorded frequently in a broad repertory which includes lightweight
encores and his own transcription of popular pieces as well as virtually every important concerto and a great deal of the chamber music
literature. Fortunately, all of his recordings have been preserved in
readily available LP editions. Of all of them, it is his first one of the
Sibelius Concerto, made with Sir Thomas Beechman in 1935, that is
most frequently singled out as an illustration of everything Heifetz's
name has stood for.

A quarter-century later Heifetz made a second recording of the
Sibelius Concerto, with the Chicago Symphony Orchestra under its
American associate conductor Walter Hendl. It, too, is superb; the
orchestral contribution is possibly even more brilliant than that of
Beecham's London Philharmonic, and the stereophonic sound is of
course far more vivid and sumptuous than that of the 1935 recording,
which was originally on 78s. But Heifetz, in his mid-thirties, showed
a degree of fiery intensity in the earlier version that was exceptional
even for him and is rare enough in a live performance, let alone a
recorded one. Perhaps he was conscious of the mission he was under-
taking in making the premiere recording of a great work that had not
received its due in the concert halls of the world. In any event, this
recording probably did more than anything else to correct that situation: it made the public familiar with the concerto, and encouraged
other violinists to learn it. Today it is an established repertory piece,
represented by more than a dozen current recordings, and several
eminent violinists have followed Heifetz's example further in recording it more than once.

Sibelius was not the sort of composer from whom one would expect
any concertos. The element of display meant very little to him, and
he was concerned in general with music whose substance determined

156

Jascha Heifetz   NYPL

its form. That his solitary concerto should be for the violin, however, need not surprise us if we trouble to learn about his early life, for when he went off to Berlin to study in his twenties, it was with the intention of becoming a virtuoso violinist himself; only then did he discover his true calling as a creator rather than a performer. As a violinist, he understood the instrument thoroughly and knew what he could demand of it; he composed a concerto whose technical difficulties are justified only by its sublime beauty, and one in which the concept is at least as truly symphonic as it is violinistic. The imaginative coloring—in the writing for both the solo instrument and the orchestra—and the superb themes were to be unsurpassed, if not unmatched, by anything Sibelius was to create afterward.

The concerto was composed in 1903 and introduced in Helsinki the following year, with Viktor Nováček as soloist and Sibelius himself conducting. Dissatisfied with the work, Sibelius undertook a substantial revision; in the premiere of the final version, given in Berlin on 19 October 1905, the soloist was Karl Halíř (a member of the Joa-

157

chim Quartet and concertmaster of the Berlin Philharmonic) and the conductor was Richard Strauss. There are more than a few nods to the great romantic-virtuoso tradition in the work, which manages nonetheless to be thoroughly and unmistakably Sibelian in every bar.

The delicate initial phrase of the first movement opens out into an impassioned theme, quite unreserved in its emotional thrust; the orchestral passages suggested to the work's early audiences such images as "bardic songs heard against a background of torches or pagan fires in some wild Northern night." The slow movement is similarly openhearted in its expressiveness, and the finale is curiously almost menacing in its vigor and brilliance. This final movement is in the form of a stylized polonaise ("evidently a polonaise for polar bears," according to Sir Donald Francis Tovey); Sibelius made a casual reference to it as a *danse macabre,* and the eerie quality of the E-string passages for the soloist and the final peroration with its terse punctuation by the blazing horns may support such a notion without further elaboration.

After World War II, Heifetz made two additional recordings with Beecham—Mozart's Concerto no. 4 in D (K. 218) and the Mendelssohn Concerto in E minor—which are together now on Seraphim 60162.

Several of his choice chamber music recordings are listed earlier in this booklet in the Rubinstein, Feuermann, and Primrose sections; RCA has gathered still more of them—Mozart's Divertimento K. 563 for string trio with Primrose and Feuermann, three Beethoven string trios with Primrose and Piatigorsky, sonatas by Mozart, Grieg, and Beethoven (Brooks Smith and Emanuel Bay alternating as pianist), and others—together in a six-disc set (CRM6-2264), and most of the other recordings he made from 1917 to 1955 in a *Heifetz Collection* comprising six four-disc sets (ARM4-0942/0947). The idea of the latter series was to restore to circulation all of Heifetz's recordings *except* the chamber music: in the six volumes are dozens of solo works— ranging from Bach partitas and Beethoven sonatas to encore pieces and Heifetz's own transcriptions—and all the big concertos as well as other concerted works, with such conductors as Toscanini, Koussevitzky, Ormandy, Steinberg, Susskind, Barbirolli, and Sargent.

Among Heifetz's stereophonic remakes of the great concertos for RCA, several have been remastered recently, either digitally or at half-speed, appreciably improving on the already good sound. The Beethoven, with Munch and the Boston Symphony Orchestra, is on

AGL1-5242. The Brahms, with Reiner and the Chicago, is on ARP1-4445. The Tchaikovsky with Reiner and the Mendelssohn with Munch are paired on ARP1-4567. A stunning account of Mozart's *Sinfonia concertante,* with William Primrose, viola, and Izler Solomon conducting, is paired with the Glazunov Concerto, Hendl conducting, on AGL1-4929.

Of the contemporary concertos Heifetz championed, Miklós Rózsa's is temporarily out of circulation, but the one by Erich Wolfgang Korngold, with Alfred Wallenstein conducting, comes with Lalo's *Symphonie espagnole* (Steinberg conducting) on AGM1-4902. Louis Gruenberg's Concerto, with Monteux conducting, has been repackaged with the marvelous performance of the Dohnányi Serenade for string trio (with Primrose and Feuermann) on AGM1-4942. The mono collection of encore pieces (LM-2382) demonstrates the charm as well as the sheer dazzle Heifetz could produce when he felt it appropriate.

It was CBS Masterworks, not RCA, that gave recorded permanence to the Los Angeles concert of 1972, in two-disc set M2-33444. Brooks Smith is the pianist in the Franck and Strauss sonatas, Ravel's *Tzigane,* and various shorter works and transcriptions. Another CBS disc offers chamber music with Piatigorsky et al. (M 33447), and some previously unreleased material from the Heifetz-Piatigorsky Concerts has turned up on another label, Vox Cum Laude: Beethoven's Piano Trio op. 70, no. 2, and Brahms's String Quintet no. 2 are on VCL-9041.

—R.F.

Richard Freed has been writing about music for more than thirty years, as a regular contributor to *Saturday Review* for thirteen years, staff critic for the *New York Times,* creator of the "Record Shelf" feature in the original Lincoln Center program magazines, and contributor to numerous other periodicals in this country and abroad. He reviewed records on the air for WEFM, Chicago, and then was record critic for the *Washington Post* for eight years; at present he is a contributing editor of both *Stereo Review* and *Opus.* Mr. Freed has written liner notes and annotative booklets for more than 300 recordings. His program annotations for three orchestras (the Philadelphia Orchestra for ten years, the National Symphony in Washington since 1977, and the St. Louis Symphony since 1973) earned him the ASCAP Deems Taylor Award in 1984. He also serves as commentator for the St. Louis Symphony's weekly broadcasts, distributed by National Public Radio, and as consultant to the music director of the National Symphony. Since 1974 he has been executive director of the Music Critics Association.

Peter Eliot Stone writes frequently about music. In addition to articles for the *New York Times, Keynote, Opera News, Symphony Magazine,* and others, he has written countless program and liner notes, as well as the entry on Antoine Reicha in the new edition of Grove's *Dictionary of Music and Musicians.* A former member of the New York State Council on the Arts, Mr. Stone studied composition with Darius Milhaud and Leon Kirchner and taught musicology at the Eastman School of Music.